$40.00
(Canada: $40.00)

RECREATIONAL COOKING

Sping, Spang, Sputter, SPLOT!

By: Janie May

From the Author:

I have enjoyed cooking since I was a child.   Enjoy is a weak word.   I have loved cooking since I was a child.   In my mid-twenties, I kicked it up a few notches and began preparing gourmet meals, learning from my mistakes and other chefs.   Practice makes perfect and cooking becomes natural.   Anybody can prepare a gourmet meal and certainly with the help of an easy to follow recipe.

I cook because I love it.   I cook to pass the time.   I cook because it is fun.   I cook because it is rewarding.   I cook solely for recreation.   I like planning meals, shopping for ingredients, and putting on my chef's jacket to begin slicing and dicing.   Proper planning and prepping before cooking is the key to any great meal.   Cooking should not involve stress.   Stress does not belong in the kitchen.

Many of my friends have urged me to open a restaurant.   Having a number of friends who actually own restaurants, I know that ownership involves 18 hour work days to make the restaurant successful.   I recently retired from my job of over 26 years as a Legal Investigator for a law firm.   Acting as Senior Chef, managing, and running a restaurant is not recreational.   Writing this book and preparing the recipes I present to you is purely recreational.   Because this is my first cookbook, and because I published using Word software (which I never use···), the critics will certainly say my use of pictures is amateur.   That is okay, and if I write another book, (BIG IF), hopefully, I can improve. This book was written for the use of my life long friends.   So be it.

My husband is from the Netherlands and he loves to eat. Because Frank is Dutch, I used the Dutch language for the various chapters of this cookbook.   Before we were married, and he was living in Holland, Frank purchased most of his meals from the Butcher and they were "ready to eat".   My largest reward is crafting a great meal and having an appreciative audience.   Frank fits that bill.   This book is ultimately for him.

Bon Appetit.
Smakelijk eten   (Dutch).

Contents

VOORGERECHTEN

Appetizers

EL GATO'S QUACAMOLE

Serves: 4 to 6

INGREDIENTS:

3 ripe avocados diced into ½" cubes

Juice of one lime

½ cup of red onion finely chopped

1 can of black beans, rinsed and drained

1 cup of frozen corn, thawed

½ cup of red pepper chopped

1 teaspoon of chili powder

½ teaspoon of cumin

1 tablespoon of cilantro chopped

Hot sauce to taste

DIRECTIONS:

In a large bowl, mix the avocados with the lime juice.   Add the remaining ingredients and mix well to distribute the spices.   Serve with your favorite tortilla chips and an ice-cold Corona. Ugly but delicious!

ASPARAGUS SPEARS IN PHYLLO

Serves: 8

INGREDIENTS:

1 bunch of asparagus, tough ends trimmed

5 slices of good quality proscuitto, cut into long strips 1" wide

2 sheets of Phyllo dough

1/4 cup of butter, melted

Grated parmesan cheese

Poppy seeds (if desired)

Chopped chives

DIRECTIONS:

Preheat oven to 375 degrees. Cut two sheets of Phyllo dough in half lengthwise. Brush the dough with half of the melted butter and sprinkle all over with parmesan cheese. Wrap two asparagus sprigs with a strip of proscuitto and then wrap the asparagus bundle with just enough of the Phyllo dough to seal the bundle. Repeat with the remaining asparagus and proscuitto. Arrange the bundles on a cookie sheet and brush all over with the remaining butter. Sprinkle the bundles with more parmesan cheese, poppy seeds, if using, and bake them for 15 minutes until the Phyllo is crispy. Sprinkle with chopped chives and serve.

PLEASE PASS THE HUMMUS
IN HONOR & MEMORY OF JUDGE BRIAN SHORTELL

Serves: 8

INGREDIENTS:

2 15-ounce cans of chick peas (garbanzo beans) – rinsed and drained

1/4 cup of Tahini paste

4 tablespoons of extra virgin olive oil

1 ½ tablespoons of fresh lemon juice

2 large garlic cloves crushed

½ teaspoon of salt

½ teaspoon of chili powder

1 tablespoon of toasted pine nuts

1 teaspoon of chopped parsley

Sprinkle of paprika

Pita bread cut into triangles

Sliced cucumbers, baby carrots, sliced red bell peppers

DIRECTIONS:

In a food processer, pulse the chick peas, Tahini paste, olive oil, lemon juice, garlic cloves, salt and chili powder until smooth and incorporated.   If the mixture is too dense, add a little more olive oil and pulse again.   Transfer the hummus to a serving dish and top with the pine nuts, parsley and paprika.   Serve on a large platter surrounded by the pita wedges and fresh vegetables.   Pour your guests a nice Chardonnay!

CHOPHOUSE STEAK TARTARE

Serves: 8

INGREDIENTS:

1 ½ pounds of high quality sirloin or filet mignon steak

1 egg yolk

2 teaspoons of Dijon mustard

2 tablespoons of capers, drained

2 tablespoons of onions, finely chopped

2 ½ teaspoons of Worcestershire sauce

3 tablespoons of extra virgin olive oil (divided)

2 teaspoons of chopped parsley

Salt and pepper to taste

Thinly sliced toasted Baguette for serving

Finely chopped onion for topping

DIRECTIONS:

Preheat the oven to 400 degrees. Slice a Baguette on the diagonal into 1/4" slices, place slices on a baking sheet and brush with some of the olive oil. Bake approximately 4 minutes. Flip the slices and bake until golden. Remove the baguette slices from the oven. In a food processor, add the beef, and next eight ingredients. Pulse until nicely incorporated, but not until the mixture forms a paste. If serving immediately, add the egg yolk and mix well. Tartare cannot be preserved for more than 2 hours, even in the refrigerator. Scrape the Tartare into a serving dish and serve with the toasted baguette and a fine Cabernet Sauvignon.

MAINE LOBSTER SALAD IN ENDIVE

Serves: 4

INGREDIENTS:

1 pound of fresh cooked lobster meat, diced small

3/4 cup of celery, diced fine

½ cup of mayonnaise

1 tablespoon of fresh dill, chopped

1 tablespoon of fresh tarragon, chopped fine

1 tablespoon of capers, drained

1 small shallot, minced (optional)

Kosher salt and freshly cracked pepper to taste

4 heads of Belgian endive, leaves separated

DIRECTIONS:

In a medium bowl, combine the lobster and next seven ingredients and mix until well incorporated. Cut the ends off the endive and separate into individual leaves. Place the lobster salad in a serving bowl and surround with the Belgian endive leaves. Have a drink! You are a Rock Star!

SAUCIJZENBROODJES
(DUTCH SAUSAGE ROLLS WITH PHYLLO DOUGH)

Serves: A crowd

INGREDIENTS:

½ pound of lean ground beef

½ pound of pork sausage

1 egg

2 tablespoons of milk

1 teaspoon of salt

1/8 teaspoon of nutmeg

Freshly ground pepper to taste

1 tablespoon of finely chopped parsley

¼ cup of Panko crumbs

1 teaspoon of Worcestershire sauce

4 sheets of Phyllo dough pastry sheets – room temperature

1 egg yolk mixed with 1 teaspoon of water

DIRECTIONS:

Preheat oven to 400 degrees.   Line a baking sheet with parchment paper and set aside.   In a large mixing bowl, gently mix together the first ten ingredients. In 16 equal portions, form the meat mixture into 5-6 inch hotdog shaped tubes. Unfold the pastry sheets.   Cut each rectangular sheet into four sheets lengthwise.   Roll each sausage in one pastry sheet. Using wet fingers, seal the edges of the sausage rolls and place on the parchment paper. With a pastry brush, brush the rolls with the egg yolk and water.   Place the baking sheet in the oven and bake for 20 minutes, turning once.   Serve warm.   I prefer to dip the rolls in mustard, but my Dutch husband thinks this is weird.

13

SALADES

Salads

HAIL KALE CAESAR SALAD

Serves: 4 to 6 as a starter course or side dish

INGREDIENTS:

1 egg coddled (see below)

3 cloves of garlic

1/2 teaspoon of sea salt

5 tablespoons of extra virgin olive oil (divided)

1 lemon or 2 limes juiced

2 teaspoons of anchovy paste (or 3 anchovies canned and diced fine)

3 drops of Worcestershire sauce

1 bunch of curly Kale, torn into bite size pieces (discard thick stalks)

Freshly grated Parmigiano Reggiano cheese

Store-bought or homemade croutons

DIRECTIONS:

In a small saucepan, bring water to a boil and add a fresh egg. Begin counting to 60 and remove egg from water. In a wooden bowl mash the garlic cloves with the sea salt. Add 2 tablespoons of the olive oil and continue mashing the garlic until it is a fine paste. Add remaining 3 tablespoons of olive oil and the juice of a lemon or limes. Add the anchovy paste or finely diced anchovies and the Worcestershire sauce. Whisk the mixture thoroughly. Add the kale and a generous handful of grated parmesan cheese, along with the croutons. Toss the salad and serve immediately.

SWEET & TANGY FRESH CORN SALAD

Serves: 4 to 6

INGREDIENTS:

4 ears of sweet corn

½ of a red onion diced

½ of a red pepper diced

2 tablespoons of extra virgin olive oil

2 tablespoons of rice wine vinegar or red wine vinegar

1 teaspoon of red Cholula sauce (in Mexican section of grocery store)

½ teaspoon of sea salt

1/3 cup chopped cilantro (optional)

Freshly cracked pepper

DIRECTIONS:

Blanch the sweet corn in boiling salted water for about 3 minutes. Remove the corn from the boiling water and place in an ice bath to stop the cooking. Dry the sweet corn on a towel. Once the corn is cool enough to handle, use a sharp knife to remove the kernels from the cob. Place the kernels in a medium to large serving dish and add the red onion, red pepper, olive oil, vinegar, cholula sauce, salt and cilantro (if using). Crack a generous amount of black pepper over the salad. Toss the salad without breaking it up into individual kernels. Serve immediately or refrigerate and serve within 2 hours. You can also make this dish in advance by leaving out the vinegar, olive oil, salt and pepper and add them when you are ready to serve.

RESTAURANT STYLE
ZESTY JAPANESE SALAD

Serves: 6

INGREDIENTS:

Dressing:

1/4 cup of minced white onion or shallots

1 small shredded carrot

1/4 cup of canola oil

4 tablespoons of rice wine vinegar

1 tablespoon of finely shredded ginger root

2 teaspoons of agave nectar

2 teaspoons of soy sauce or ponzu sauce

1 tablespoon of ketchup

1 teaspoon of lemon or lime juice

1/4 teaspoon of salt

Salad:

1 small head of Iceberg lettuce chopped large

1 large shredded carrot

DIRECTIONS:

In a small immersion blender, blend all of the dressing ingredients until well mixed. In 6 small bowls, arrange the chopped iceberg lettuce and top each salad with the shredded carrot. Top each salad with an equal amount of the dressing.

FRESH RASPBERRY SALAD

(Courtesy of my good friend, Victoria Blower)

Serves: 4

INGREDIENTS:

Dressing:

½ cup Canola oil

1 ½ tablespoons of Agave nectar or Truvia

2 tablespoons of raspberry vinegar

1 tablespoon of fresh lemon juice

1 tablespoon of sour cream or plain yogurt

1 tablespoon of poppy seeds

1 ½ tablespoons of Framboise raspberry liqueur

Salt & Pepper

Salad:

Assorted greens

Chopped walnuts or pecans

1 pint of fresh raspberries

DIRECTIONS:

In a mason jar, add the oil, agave or sugar-substitute, vinegar and lemon juice and shake well. Add the additional dressing ingredients and whisk well. In a large bowl, mix the greens with the walnuts and raspberries. Add the dressing and toss gently. Divide salad amongst four plates and serve.

My best friend, Dr. Victoria (Vicky) Blower, and my sister, Gwen, decorating for our wedding.

FRENCH SALADE LYONNAISE

Serves: 2

INGREDIENTS:

2 cups of mixed salad greens

2 cups of Arugula

6 strips of thick peppered bacon cooked to desire and torn into pieces

1/4 of a small red onion sliced very thin

Buttered croutons - homemade or store bought

2 tablespoons of extra virgin olive oil

3 tablespoons of red wine vinegar

1 teaspoon of Dijon mustard

Salt and freshly cracked pepper to taste

2 large eggs

DIRECTIONS:

Arrange half of the greens and arugula in each of two large shallow salad bowls or pasta dishes.   To each bowl, add half of the bacon, red onion and croutons.   Mix together the olive oil, red wine vinegar, mustard and salt to taste.   Either fry the eggs in butter or poach the eggs in water until cooked to your desire and carefully drain on paper towels.   Top each salad with a fried or poached egg and freshly cracked pepper.   Enjoy with a freshly made Mimosa!

CLUB HOUSE WEDGE SALAD

Serves: 4

INGREDIENTS:
DRESSING:
1/4 cup of olive oil
1/4 cup of red wine vinegar
1 tablespoon of soy sauce
1 packet of Truvia sweetener
½ teaspoon of oregano
Freshly cracked pepper to taste

SALAD:
1 crisp head of iceberg lettuce, core removed, quartered and rinsed
1 cup of crumbled gorgonzola cheese
1 large tomato diced
8 slices of cooked bacon, crumbled (optional)

Whisk the dressing ingredients thoroughly and set aside. Arrange the lettuce quarters on four plates and top with the gorgonzola crumbles, tomato and bacon (if using). Dress each salad with a quarter of the dressing and serve.

SAVORY SPINACH & CREAMY GORGONZOLA SALAD

Serves: 6

INGREDIENTS:

Dressing:

½ cup of extra virgin olive oil

1 shallot minced

4 tablespoons of red Port (or good red wine)

1 tablespoon good quality balsamic vinegar

1 tablespoon of honey or agave nectar

Salad:

2 bags of fresh spinach

Crumbled gorgonzola cheese

Crumbled cooked bacon (optional)

DIRECTIONS:

Heat the oil in a skillet until hot but not smoking, and add the minced shallot, cooking until the shallots are soft about 1 minute. Pour oil mixture in a small bowl. Add the port, vinegar and honey or nectar and whisk well. In a salad bowl, add the spinach, top with the crumbled gorgonzola cheese and bacon if using. Toss the salad with the dressing. To make this in advance, keep the dressing separate and toss when you are ready to serve.

GREEK SALAD WITH BLACKENED CHICKEN

Serves: 2

INGREDIENTS:

Dressing:

1/4 cup of olive oil

1/4 cup of red wine vinegar

1 packet of Truvia sweetener

½ teaspoon of oregano

Freshly cracked pepper to taste

Salad:

1 small head of iceberg lettuce or 1 bunch of romaine

1 large ripe tomato cut into bite size pieces

1/4 of an English cucumber chopped or sliced

½ of a red or green pepper sliced into bite size pieces

1 handful of Kalamata olives sliced in half

4 ounces of Feta cheese broken into bite size pieces

1 tablespoon of thinly sliced red onion

2 chicken breasts pounded to an even thickness of 3/4"

Olive oil spray in a can

Blackening seasoning:

1 tablespoon of paprika

2 teaspoons of garlic powder

2 teaspoons of onion powder

1 teaspoon of ground black pepper

1 teaspoon of dried thyme

1 teaspoon of cayenne powder

1 teaspoon of salt

½ teaspoon of ground coriander

DIRECTIONS:

Mix all salad dressing ingredients in a mason jar and let sit for 1 to 2 hours to blend the flavors. Make the salad and refrigerate. Mix together the blackening season and crush with a mortar and pestle to break down the thyme. Spray the chicken breasts with the olive oil spray and generously sprinkle with the blackening seasoning on both sides. You will have seasoning left over for future meals. Grill the breasts until nice browned and cooked through. Let the breasts rest under foil for 5 minutes. Toss the salad with the dressing and divide between two bowls. Slice each chicken breast and place one on top of each salad. Light and yummy!

GINGER SESAME ASIAN SLAW

Serves: 4

INGREDIENTS:

1 ½ tablespoons of toasted sesame seeds (just until golden)

4 ½ cups of cabbage sliced thin

1 cup of carrot cut into matchsticks pieces

½ cup of green onions thinly cut on the diagonal

2 tablespoons of canola oil

3 tablespoons of rice wine vinegar (unseasoned)

½ teaspoon of agave nectar

1 ½ tablespoons of finely grated ginger

½ teaspoon of sesame oil

DIRECTIONS:

Toast sesame seeds in a small skillet, stirring frequently being careful not to burn them.

In a large bowl, add cabbage, carrot and green onions. In a mason jar, combine the oil, vinegar, agave nectar, ginger and sesame oil and shake vigorously until well mixed. Add the dressing and sesame seeds to the salad and toss to incorporate flavors. Slaw can be made an hour in advance and refrigerated until serving.

FRANK'S BACON SPINACH SALAD

Serves: 2 as a light lunch

INGREDIENTS:

3 medium boiled eggs (yolks should have an orange color) 7 minutes

3 tablespoons of sugar or 1 ½ tablespoons of agave nectar

3 tablespoons of white vinegar

1 ½ teaspoon of Dijon mustard

1 bag of spinach (16 ounces)

4-5 slices of cooked thick peppered bacon, cooked and chopped

1 tablespoon of bacon grease

2 green onions chopped

½ cup of toasted pine nuts

DIRECTIONS:

Cut boiled eggs in half and remove the yolks, reserving the egg whites. In a small bowl, combine the egg yolks with the sugar or nectar, vinegar and Dijon mustard until well mixed. In a bowl, toss the spinach with the dressing. Add the bacon grease and toss again. Top the salad with chopped egg whites, onions, pine nuts and bacon.

TANGY ENGLISH CUCUMBER SALAD

Serves: 4

INGREDIENTS:

1 long English cucumber

1 small sweet onion sliced thinly into rounds

3 tablespoons of cider vinegar (or substitute white vinegar)

2 teaspoons of Agave Nectar or sugar substitute

½ teaspoon of salt

1 teaspoon of fresh cracked pepper

2-3 tablespoons of fresh dill chopped

DIRECTIONS:

Using a sharp vegetable peeler, cut strips from the English cucumber leaving thin strips of green peel on the cucumber. Slice the cucumber into 1/8" slices and place in a salad bowl. Break up the onion rounds and add to the cucumber. In a small bowl, whisk together the cider vinegar, Agave Nectar (or sugar substitute), salt and pepper until well incorporated and the sugar and salt are dissolved. Add the chopped dill to the cucumbers and onion. Add the dressing to the cucumber bowl and mix well to blend the cucumbers with the onion. Refrigerate for an hour and up to two hours to blend the flavors.

CAPRESE SALAD WITH TOASTED BAQUETTE

Serves: 8 as an appetizer or first course

INGREDIENTS:

1 fresh loaf of baguette bread sliced on a diagonal into ½" slices

Spray olive oil in the can

8 Roma tomatoes cut into generous quarter inch slices

1 one pound log of fresh mozzarella cheese

1 package of basil leaves (large leaves torn in half)

½ of a red onion sliced very thin

Extra virgin olive oil for drizzling

High quality balsamic vinegar for drizzling (I prefer Di Modena balsamic vinegar from the St. Helena Olive Oil Co. in Napa Valley)

Freshly cracked black pepper

DIRECTIONS:

Preheat oven to 375 degrees. Place the sliced baguettes on a cooking sheet. Spray one side lightly with the oil. Toast the baguettes in the oven until lightly golden on one side and then flip and toast the other side watching them carefully so they do not burn. Remove and take off the cooking sheet and transfer to a lined serving basket. On a long decorative platter beginning at one end, begin overlapping the next three ingredients in this order: tomato, basil, cheese, basil and then tomato again. Repeat until your tray is completely full. Sprinkle the sliced red onion over the top. Just before serving, drizzle with the olive oil and balsamic vinegar to taste. Crack the fresh pepper over the top and serve with the baguettes. The salad is best at room temperature with a nice bottle of Chianti.

Caprese Salad recipe

CHOPPED SALAD WITH GOAT CHEESE MEDALLIONS

Serves: 4 as a light lunch

INGREDIENTS:

1/2 cup of light olive oil

4 tablespoons of red wine vinegar

Juice of one lemon

2 teaspoons of dijon mustard

3 heads of romaine lettuce rinsed, dried and cut into bite sized pieces

2 medium heirloom tomatoes chopped

½ of a red onion sliced thin

2 ribs of celery sliced

2 tablespoons of olive oil

1 six ounce log of goat cheese sliced into generous ½" slices (12 total)

2 beaten eggs

1 cup panko crumbs

½ cup of toasted slivered almonds

½ cup of dried cherries or cranberries

DIRECTIONS:

In a mason jar, mix the first four ingredients until the mustard is incorporated. Place the lettuce in a large salad bowl, add the tomatoes, onion, and celery and toss with the dressing. Set aside. Heat the olive oil in a skillet over medium heat. Dip the goat cheese slices in the beaten egg and then into the panko crumbs. When the oil is hot, but not smoking, add the breaded goat cheese to the skillet and cook until golden brown on one side. Flip and brown the other side. Arrange the salad on each of four generous salad bowls. Top each salad with equal amount of the almonds and cherries. Top each salad with three goat cheese rounds and serve immediately.

RUNDVLEES

Beef

PERFECTLY GRILLED TENDERLOIN STEAKS
WITH COFFEE COCOA RUB
(Also good on Ribeye Steaks)

Serves: 4

INGREDIENTS:

(Recipe makes more than you will use on 4 steaks)

4   2 ½ " thick Filet Mignon steaks

1 ½ tablespoons of whole coriander seeds

1/3 cup freshly ground coffee

1/4 cup cocoa powder

3 tablespoons of brown sugar

1 tablespoon of kosher salt

1 tablespoon of freshly cracked pepper

1 tablespoon of smoked paprika

2 teaspoons of onion powder

1 teaspoon of garlic powder

Canola oil

DIRECTIONS:

Ground coriander seed with a mortar and pestle, or in a spice grinder until broken down but not a fine dust.   In a small bowl, mix coriander, coffee, cocoa powder, brown sugar, salt, cracked pepper, paprika, onion powder and garlic powder until well incorporated.   Rub Canola oil on all sides of the steaks.   Generously sprinkle rub onto all sides of the steaks (the steaks should be coated with rub) and press the rub into the meat.   Prior to grilling the steaks, let them sit at room temperature for 30 minutes.   Heat a gas grill to high heat and oil the grates of the grill (being careful not to burn yourself - oil plus heat equals fire.....).   Once grill is at 400 degrees covered, place steaks on grill and grill to desired doneness.   I like my steaks medium rare to rare and a 2 1/2 inch steak on a hot grill takes about 5 minutes per side uncovered.   Adjust cooking time to your desired degree of doneness and the heat of your grill.   The steaks can also be cooked in an oiled cast iron skillet in the same fashion. Remove steaks and cover loosely with foil and let them rest 5 minutes to retain the juices.

DECADENT BEEF STROGANOFF

Serves: 6

INGREDIENTS:

2 pounds of cooked leftover pot roast cut into cubes

3 tablespoons of olive oil

2 medium sweet onions or white onions sliced thin

4 cloves of garlic chopped

8 ounces of quartered large button mushrooms

8 ounces of halved cremini mushroom

½ cup of butter

½ cup of Sherry

½ cup of flour

4 cups unsalted beef stock

2 beef bouillon cubes (I use Knorrs)

1 teaspoon of salt

Freshly cracked pepper to taste

2 teaspoons of worcestershire sauce

2 cups of sour cream

2 tablespoons of flat leaf parsley chopped

2 tablespoons of fresh dill chopped

Hot cooked lightly buttered egg noodles sprinkled with poppy seeds

DIRECTIONS:

Saute the onions in the olive oil on medium high heat in a Dutch oven on the stove until limp and translucent (about 10 minutes), stirring frequently. Add the garlic to the onions and saute about 1 minute longer. Remove onions and garlic from the pan and place in a large bowl - set aside. Melt butter in the same pan and add the mushrooms and saute until golden brown. Remove the mushrooms to the bowl with the onions. Add the sherry and cook over medium heat, scraping up any brown bits on the bottom of the pan. Continue cooking until sherry is reduced by half. Add the onions and mushrooms back to the pan. Add the flour and stir into the onion and mushroom mixture. Add the beef stock, boullion, cubed pot roast, salt, a generous amount of fresh cracked pepper and the worcestershire sauce. Bring to a boil and cook until thickened. Lower the heat to low. Stir in sour cream, parsley and dill and simmer over low heat until heated through. Serve over the buttered and poppy seed egg noodles. This is one of my husband's favorite recipes!

IRRESISTIBLE SOY MARINATED FLANK STEAK

Serves: 5-6

INGREDIENTS:

3 Leeks (white to light green part only), thoroughly washed and cut into thin rings

½ cup of Soy Sauce

1/4 cup of orange juice

3 tablespoons of olive or canola oil

2 limes juiced

1 ½ tablespoons of Agave Nectar or brown sugar

1 teaspoon of sesame oil

1 teaspoon of hot red pepper flakes

2 or 3 pound Flank steak

Freshly cracked course pepper

DIRECTIONS:

In a bowl, combine the leeks, soy sauce, orange juice, oil, lime juice, agave nectar or brown sugar, sesame oil and red pepper flakes. Wisk to incorporate the flavors. Make shallow cuts in the flank steak in two directions on a diagonal on both sides. Place the flank steak in a large zip lock bag or 9 x 13 glass dish. Pour marinade over steak and flip a time or two. Cover with saran wrap and marinate for 4 hours or overnight (preferred). Remove steak from the marinade and generously coat with freshly cracked pepper. Grill steak on a hot oiled grill for about 4 to 5 minutes per side depending on the thickness of your flank steak. You want a nice sear and your meat should be pink in the center. Place the flank steak on a large platter and cover loosely with foil. Let it rest for 5 minutes. Place steak on a large cutting board and cut it at an angle into slices across the grain of the meat. I like it cut about 1/4 inch thick, but suit yourself.

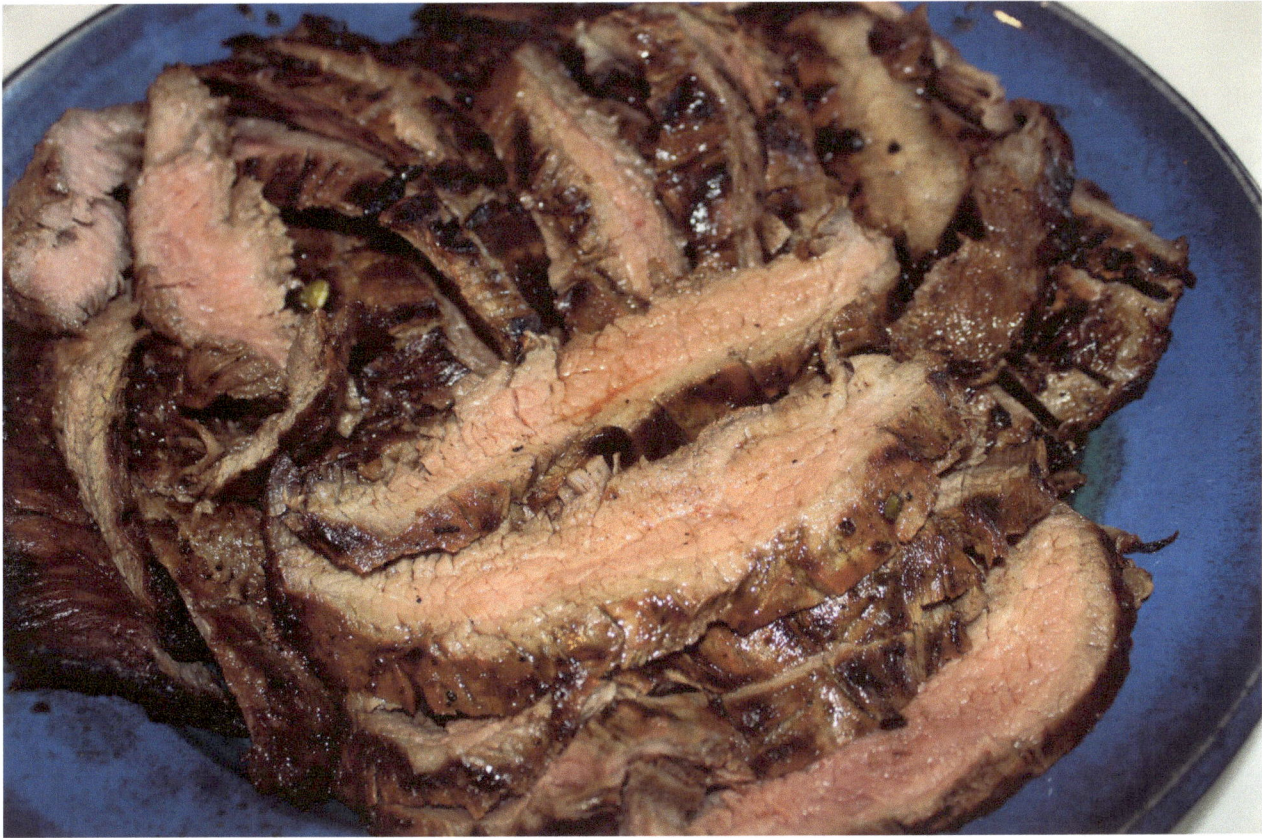

SIZZLIN' STIR-FRIED ASIAN BEEF & NOODLES

Serves: 4

INGREDIENTS:

6 ounces of wide rice noodles (Asian aisle of the grocery store)

1 teaspoon of Shiracha chile sauce

½ of an orange juiced

2 tablespoons of unseasoned rice wine vinegar

2 tablespoons of soy sauce

1 tablespoon of Asian fish sauce

1 ½ tablespoons of grate ginger

1 packet of Stevia sweetener

1 teaspoon of sesame oil

3 tablespoons of coconut oil or canola oil

1 ½ pounds of sirloin or ribeye steak sliced 1/8" thick (or pork)

3 cloves of garlic sliced thin

12 ounces of oyster mushrooms (or button mushrooms if preferred)

4 cups of chopped baby kale

3/4 cup of thickly sliced green onions - green and white parts

½ of a red pepper sliced (optional)

½ cup of cilantro chopped

DIRECTIONS:

Cook the rice noodles according to the package directions, drain and rinse to stop the cooking. In a small bowl, add the Siracha, orange juice, vinegar, soy sauce, fish sauce, ginger, Stevia and sesame oil. Whisk until incorporated.   Set the mixture aside.   Add the oil to a wok and heat over high heat.   Add the steak and brown quickly on all sides.   Remove the steak and add the mushrooms to the pan. Cook until golden brown. Add the garlic and stir-fry one minute.   Add the baby kale, green onion, red pepper and stir fry until the kale is just wilted.   Return the steak to the pan and add the sauce mixture.   Stir-fry to incorporate. Add the noodles and stir fry until heated through. Top with the cilantro and serve immediately.

RESTAURANT-STYLE
CHINESE GREEN PEPPER STEAK

Serves: 4

INGREDIENTS:

1/4 cup soy sauce

1 tablespoon oyster sauce

2 packets Truvia sweetener or 1 tablespoon Agave Nectar

1 teaspoon of freshly cracked pepper

1 teaspoon Siracha sauce

5 drops of sesame oil

1 ½ pounds sirloin steak cut into strips about ½" thick

1 sweet onion cut into ½" slices

2 green bell peppers cut into ½" slices

3 to 4 tablespoons of canola oil

½ cup of beef stock mixed with ½ teaspoon of cornstarch

Brown rice

DIRECTIONS:

In a small bowl, whisk the soy sauce, oyster sauce, Truvia, pepper, Siracha sauce and sesame oil.   Place the sirloin steak in a bowl, pour the marinade over the top and mix with your hands to incorporate.   Marinate a couple of hours and remove the meat from the marinade, reserving the marinade.   In a wok or large skillet, heat two tablespoons of the oil over medium high heat until hot but not smoking.   Add half of the steak and stir fry until nicely browned. Remove the cooked beef to a plate and repeat with the remaining steak, adding more oil if necessary.   Reduce the heat to medium and add the onions and more oil if necessary and cook until done but not limp. Add the green pepper and stir fry about 3 minutes.   Return the steak to the pan and stir fry with the onions and peppers 3 minutes.   Add the reserved marinade and the beef stock mixed with cornstarch and stir until bubbly and slightly thickened.   Serve over brown rice.

WINE BRAISED SHORT RIBS OVER PASTA

Serves: 4

INGREDIENTS:

8 Beefy bone-in short ribs

Salt & freshly cracked pepper

1-2 tablespoons of canola oil

2 large sweet onions chopped

3 stalks of celery chopped

3 medium-sized carrots chopped

4 large cloves of garlic, left whole

6 large sprigs of thyme

3 sprigs of rosemary

2 tablespoons of flour

3 tablespoons of tomato paste

1 quality bottle of cabernet sauvignon

4 cups of low-sodium beef stock

4 bay leaves

12 ounces of wide egg noodles

DIRECTIONS:

Preheat oven to 350 degrees. Generously salt and pepper the short ribs all over. Heat oil in a Dutch oven over high heat and when oil is hot (not smoking), add the short ribs and brown all sides. The browning is a key step to obtain a rich taste in the stock. Remove short ribs from the pan and set aside. Reduce the heat in the pan to medium and add the onions, celery, carrots, garlic cloves, thyme and rosemary. Saute the vegetable mixture for approximately 20 minutes, stirring frequently. Add the flour and continue cooking the vegetables, stirring, for about 2 minutes. Add the tomato paste, wine, beef stock and bay leaves and stir, scraping any brown bits on the bottom of the pan, until the flour and paste have broken down and the broth is smooth, and bring to a boil for about 4 minutes. Add the short ribs to the Dutch oven and cover the pan. Put the pan in the pre-heated oven and cook for 2 hours. Uncover the pan after two hours and cook an additional 30 minutes. Remove pan from the oven and carefully remove the short ribs to a glass baking dish. Pour the sauce through a strainer into a bowl to remove the vegetables and herbs. Increase oven temperature to 400 degrees. Pour the sauce back into the Dutch oven and bring to a boil over medium high heat. Boil for approximately 30 minutes until the sauce has reduced by about half. Spoon about a cup of the sauce over the short ribs and place them in the oven for about 20 minutes and remove from oven. To plate the dish, spoon some of the sauce from the Dutch oven over a serving size portion of wide egg noodles and top with two short ribs. Serve with fresh green beans and a mixed green salad.

KAFTA (DELICIOUS LEBANESE BEEF KABOBS)

Serves: 6 to 8

KABOB INGREDIENTS:

2 pounds of low fat ground beef

½ grated sweet onion

3 tablespoons of finely chopped large leaf parsley

½ teaspoon of allspice

½ teaspoon of cinnamon

½ teaspoon of cumin

½ teaspoon of ground coriander

½ teaspoon of cayenne pepper

½ teaspoon of fine sea salt

½ teaspoon of freshly ground black pepper

2 tablespoons of canola oil

8 wooden skewers soaked in water for 30 minutes

SAUCE:

1 cup of plain greek style yogurt

1 teaspoon of cumin

½ of an English cucumber grated

Juice of ½ lemon

1 clove of garlic minced

1/2 teaspoon crushed red pepper

1/4 teaspoon salt

Pita Bread

DIRECTIONS:

Mix the ground beef with all of the ingredients except the oil, mixing with your hands. Try not to over-mix the beef or the kabobs will be dense and less juicy when cooked. Divide meat into quarter pound portions and form the beef mixture into 8 sausage shapes. Skewer each sausage with the wooden skewers. Brush the kabobs with the canola oil. Mix the yogurt with the remaining ingredients to make a sauce.   Heat a gas grill on high heat to 400 degrees.   Cook the kabobs on an oiled grill, turning frequently (but sear the first side down about 3 minutes or you will have trouble turning the kabobs - use a metal spatula if needed), until browned and cooked through, about 20 minutes uncovered.   Remove kabobs from grill and cover loosely with foil for about 5 minutes to rest. Serve with warm pita bread, the sauce, and a mixed green salad.

LA COCINA CARNE ASADA

Serves: 6

INGREDIENTS:

2 pounds of flank steak (or skirt steak)

½ cup of soy sauce

1/3 cup of white vinegar

3 tablespoons of fresh lime juice

Juice of ½ and orange

3 cloves of garlic, minced

2 teaspoons of black pepper

1 teaspoon of ground cumin

1 teaspoon of oregano

½ teaspoon of chili powder

½ teaspoon of cayenne pepper

DIRECTIONS:

Remove excess fat from the steak and score diagonally with 1/8" cuts to allow the marinade to penetrate.   In a small bowl, mix the remaining ingredients until well incorporated.   Place the steak in a glass dish large enough to allow the steak to lay flat.   Pour marinade over steak and marinate for 4 to 8 hours.   Remove the steak from the marinade.   Heat the grill to 400 degrees.   Grill the flank steak until nicely charred on both sides and cooked through, about 10 minutes total depending upon the thickness.   Serve with flour tortillas, sliced onion, green pepper, crisp lettuce, sour cream, salsa and limes.

HOMEMADE FIESTA TACOS

Serves: 4

INGREDIENTS:

Mix the following spices in a small dish:

1 Tablespoon Chili Powder, ¼ teaspoon garlic powder, ¼ teaspoon onion powder, pinch of cayenne pepper, ¼ teaspoon oregano, ½ teaspoon paprika, 1 ½ teaspoons ground cumin, 1 teaspoon salt

2/3 cup of water

1 pound of lean ground beef

10 Crispy taco shells

Shredded cheddar cheese

Shredded iceberg lettuce

Diced tomatoes

Sour Cream and Salsa

DIRECTIONS:

Brown the ground beef in a skillet and drain. Add the spice blend and 2/3 cup of water. Bring beef and sauce to a boil. Reduce heat and simmer for 5 minutes. Divide the meat mixture between the taco shells and top with the cheese, lettuce, and tomatoes. Serve with the sour cream and salsa.

KICK-ASS SHORT RIB TACOS

Serves: 6

INGREDIENTS:

2 whole chipotle chiles dried

3 garlic cloves chopped

1 medium sweet onion

2 cups of chicken or beef broth

½ cup dry red wine

1 tablespoon of white vinegar

1/4 cup of brown sugar

1 teaspoon of salt

1 teaspoon of cracked black pepper

1 tablespoon of coffee cocoa rub (see page 40)

5-6 pounds of meaty beef short ribs (about 4" to 5" long & 3" wide)

2 tablespoons of canola oil

1 cinnamon stick

½ tsp. cumin

Small flour tortillas

Sour cream

Salsa

Fresh cilantro chopped

Thinly sliced sweet onion

Thinly sliced cabbage

DIRECTIONS:

Add the chipotle chiles to a small saucepan of boiling water and let boil for 18 minutes until softened. Discard the liquid and let chiles cool enough to handle. Remove stem tops, cut in half length wise and remove ribs and seeds. Dice the chiles and add to a blender. To the blender add the next 8 ingredients (through the cracked black pepper) and pulse until smooth.

Season the ribs all over with salt, pepper and coffee cocoa rub.   Heat the oil in a 12-inch saute pan over medium-high heat and add one-half of the ribs.   Brown the ribs on all sides (obtaining a nice sear on the ribs is key to this recipe).   Remove the ribs and brown the second batch.   When done, add all of the ribs to a slow cooker and cover them with the blended sauce (ribs do not need to be completely submerged in the sauce.   Add the cinnamon stick and cumin.   Cover the crock pot and cook the ribs on high for 5 hours and then turn the heat down to low for 3 hours.   The ribs are done when the meat is tender and just starting to fall off the bone.   Remove the ribs from the sauce to cool and de-grease the sauce, discarding the grease. Discard most of the sauce, leaving about one cup in the crock pot.   When the rib bones are cool enough to handle, remove the meat from the bones and cut off and discard as much fat as possible.   Add the meat to a bowl and shred with two forks.   Transfer the meat to the crock pot and mix with the sauce. Season with salt and pepper if needed. Leave crock pot on low while preparing the tortillas.   In a small skillet on medium high heat, heat each tortilla until lightly golden on one-side.   Remove tortilla and place on a piece of tinfoil.   Repeat with remaining tortillas and cover to keep warm.   Serve the beef with warm tortillas, sour cream, salsa, cilantro, onion and cabbage.   Enjoy!

MOMMA'S STUFFED BELL PEPPERS
WITH CREAMY MASHED POTATOES

Serves: 5 or more depending on appetites!

INGREDIENTS:

5 large green bell peppers or 6 medium bell peppers, tops removed

2 cups of cooked white rice made according to package

2 pounds of lean ground beef

2 teaspoons of fine sea salt

2 teaspoons of fine black pepper

½ teaspoon of onion powder

3/4 cup of Gorgonzola or bleu cheese (pick your favorite)

1 32 ounce can of whole tomatoes

1 tablespoon of fresh rosemary chopped

Freshly cracked pepper

1 32 ounce can of tomato sauce

DIRECTIONS:

Preheat the oven to 350 degrees. Wash the green peppers and dry them. Cut off the tops of the green peppers, remove the seeds and white membrane. In a large mixing bowl, mix the cooked white rice with ground beef, gorgonzola, onion powder, sea salt and pepper. Until evenly incorporated without over-working the meat. Pack the meat mixture into each green pepper and stand the peppers up with the meat on top in a Dutch oven. Pour the whole tomatoes and tomato sauce in a bowl with the fresh rosemary and crush with your hands to break up the tomatoes. Generously season with fresh cracked pepper. Pour the crushed tomato mixture over the peppers. Cover the Dutch oven and place in the oven for three hours. Let cool for several minutes before serving. Serve with your favorite creamy mashed potatoes and crusty bread. Take a nap.

LAM

Lamb

BALSAMIC MARINATED RACK OF LAMB

Serves: 2

INGREDIENTS:

1/4 cup of Ponzu sauce (in the Asian aisle of the grocery store)

1/4 cup of quality balsamic vinegar

2 tablespoons of brown sugar

2 tablespoons of lemon grass in a tube (produce section)

1 rack of lamb, frenched by the butcher or excess fat removed

2 tablespoons of olive oil

DIRECTIONS:

Remove all sinew from the rack of lamb and cut off any excess fat, leaving 1/8 of an inch of fat on the lamb.   In a large zip lock bag, mix the ponzu, vinegar, brown sugar and lemon grass. Place the rack of lamb in the bag and remove any excess air.   Marinate the lamb in the refrigerator overnight, or for at least 8 hours.   Remove the lamb from the marinade and dry off with paper towels.   Preheat the oven to 400 degrees.   Heat the olive oil in a cast iron skillet until hot over medium high heat.   Add the lamb and brown both sides (about 5 minutes per side).   Place the skillet in the preheated oven, turning on your oven fan, and cook for 15 minutes for medium rare.

ST. HELENA OLIVE OIL CO.
NAPA VALLEY
EST. 1994

BVT
balsamic
vinegar
TRADIZIONALE

ORIGIN
MODENA ITALY

FLAVOR PROFILE
BRIGHT, DENSE
AND SWEET

VARIETAL
TREBIANNO GRAPE

PRODUCTION/DATE
20 CASES
2/12/15

WWW.SHOLIVEOIL.COM

CITRUS HONEY GRILLED RACK OF LAMB

Serves: 2

INGREDIENTS:

1 Rack of lamb frenched, excess fat removed

½ cup of olive oil

½   cup of orange juice

1/4 cup of soy sauce

2 tablespoons of fresh thyme leaves chopped

2 tablespoons of honey

1 teaspoon of sea salt

Freshly cracked pepper

DIRECTIONS:

Thoroughly whisk the olive oil, juice, soy sauce, thyme, honey and salt.   In a large re-sealable plastic bag marinate the lamb rack with the sauce for 8 hours or overnight.   Preheat a gas grill to 400 degrees.   Remove lamb from the marinade.   Crack fresh pepper liberally over the lamb.   Tightly wrap the bone ends with heavy duty tin foil to keep them from burning.   Place the lamb on the grill and cook uncovered for approximately 10 minutes per side for medium rare.   Cooking time varies depending upon your gas grill.

MARINATED & PERFECTLY GRILLED
BUTTERFLIED LEG OF LAMB

Serves: 8

INGREDIENTS:

1 bunch of green onions sliced thick

4 cloves of garlic chopped

3 tablespoons of chopped fresh rosemary

Zest of one large orange

3 tablespoons of olive oil

1 tablespoon of white vinegar or apple cider vinegar

2 teaspoons of sea salt

1 tablespoon of freshly cracked pepper

1 butterflied boneless leg of lamb excess fat removed (cut through lamb and open like a book so that the lamb has an even thickness all over)

DIRECTIONS:

Place the onions, garlic, rosemary, orange zest, olive oil and vinegar in a food processor and pulse until well incorporated and smooth. Add the mixture to a large zip lock bag. Season the lamb all over with the salt and pepper and add to the zip lock, removing any excess air. Marinate the lamb overnight or for at least 8 hours. Remove the lamb from the zip lock and let it come to room temperature (about 30 minutes). Heat a gas grill on high heat. When the grill temperature is 400 degrees, place the lamb directly on the grill and grill uncovered for about 5 minutes per side. Use a water bottle or beer to put out flare-ups while the lamb is cooking. Lower the heat to low and cover the grill maintaining a temperature of 300 to 325 degrees, checking on the lamb occasionally for flare-ups. Let the lamb cook for about 20 minutes per side until a meat thermometer in the thickest part of the meat registers 130 degrees for medium rare. Transfer the leg of lamb to a cutting board and cover loosely with foil for about 7 minutes. Slice the lamb across the grain into ½ inch slices and serve.

MOUTH-WATERING GRILLED LAMB CHOPS

Serves: 6

INGREDIENTS:

12 thick cut lamb chops (about 2 inches thick)

1 tablespoon of canola oil

Salt and freshly cracked pepper

2 tablespoons of olive oil

3 tablespoons of soy sauce

1 tablespoon of brown sugar

2 tablespoons of grated fresh ginger (or ginger in the tube)

1 teaspoon of red hot sauce

DIRECTIONS:

Let the lamb sit at room temperature for approximately 25 minutes. Whisk the olive oil, soy sauce, brown sugar, ginger and hot sauce in a small bowl. Heat a gas grill on high heat until the grill temperature is 400 degrees. Rub the lamb chops all over with the canola oil. Salt and pepper both side of the chops. Place the chops on the hot grill and grill uncovered for 2 minutes per side until they are starting to lightly brown. Baste the chops with the sauce and flip them so they are sauce side down on the grill. Baste the other side of the chops. Cook the chops for about 3 to 5 minutes per side, continually basting with the sauce. Cover loosely with foil for about 3 minutes and serve immediately.

GEVOGELTE

Poultry

CITRUS GINGER CHICKEN NOODLE SALAD

Serves: 6 to 8

INGREDIENTS:

Dressing:

1/3 cup of crunchy peanut butter (or smooth)

1/4 cup of soy sauce

2 tablespoons of unseasoned rice vinegar

2 teaspoons of chile paste (such as Sambal Oelek)

2 teaspoons of brown sugar

2 tablespoons of freshly grated ginger

A good pinch of red pepper flakes

2 tablespoons of fresh squeezed lime juice

Juice of one orange

Salt and pepper to taste

Salad:

2 cups of iceberg lettuce chopped

1 16 ounce package of fresh Asian noodles (produce section)

3 cups of cooked chicken shredded

1 shredded large carrot

2 green onions sliced thinly on the diagonal

½ of a red bell pepper sliced into 2" strips

1/4 cup of cilantro chopped

½ cup of mint chopped

½ cup of lightly salted roasted peanuts or cashews

DIRECTIONS:

Place all of the dressing ingredients in a blender and blend until smooth.   If the dressing is too thick, you can thin it out with a little water or chicken broth.   For the salad, prepare the noodles according to the package (without the seasoning packet), rinse with cold water to cool and drain.   In a large bowl, toss all of the salad ingredients with the dressing.   Sprinkle with the peanuts or cashews and serve.

HAPPY BELLY CHICKEN POT PIE

Serves: 6 to 8

INGREDIENTS:

2 store-bought pie crusts at room temperature

1/3 cup of unsalted butter

1 medium sweet onion chopped

2 stalks of celery chopped

2 carrots sliced ½" thick

1 cup of potato diced into one inch cubes

2 sprigs of rosemary chopped fine

1 teaspoon of sea salt

1/4 cup of good quality drinking sherry

½ cup of flour

2 cups of low sodium chicken stock

1 cup of half and half

1 cup of frozen peas defrosted under cold water

Freshly cracked pepper

3-4 cups of cooked chicken chopped into generous bite-size pieces

1 egg whisked

DIRECTIONS:

Preheat oven to 400 degrees.   In large skillet, melt the butter over medium heat.   Add the onion, celery, carrots, potato, rosemary and sea salt and saute until the vegetables are cooked, about 10 minutes.   Add the Sherry and continue cooking until almost evaporated. Add the flour and cook the vegetables about 2 minutes longer. Add the peas.   Combine the chicken stock and half and half.   Gradually stir the broth mixture into the vegetables, stirring constantly until the mixture comes to a light boil and is thickened. Add the chicken.   Season with salt and pepper.   Pour the mixture into a lightly greased 2 quart round casserole dish. Top with the 2 pie crusts, crimp the edges to seal and make four or five decorative slits in the crusts.   Bake for 25 minutes.   Brush the pastry with the whisked egg and continue to cook the pie for 15 minutes until the pastry is golden brown and the filling is bubbly and hot.

BBQ SPATCHCOCK CORNISH GAMES HENS

Serves: 2

INGREDIENTS:

Brine:

1 cup of water

½ cup of Chardonnay

2 tablespoons of course salt

1 teaspoon of whole coriander

1 teaspoon of black peppercorns

2 cups of ice

2 Cornish game hens cleaned

Canola or olive oil spray

Cocoa Coffee Rub - see page 40

Sliced green onions

Grilled orange slices

DIRECTIONS:

Place all of the brine ingredients in a medium saucepan and bring to a boil. Let the brine simmer for 15 minutes, remove it from the stove, and then add the ice cubes to cool the brine. To spatchcock the hens, remove the backbone using kitchen shears. Flatten the hens, by pressing down on them to break the breast bone.   Brine the hens overnight in the refrigerator. When ready to grill, remove the hens from the brine, rinse with water and pat them dry.   Spray the hens with Canola oil and then generously rub them with the cocoa coffee rub.   Grill the hens on a hot covered grill for 5 minutes.   After five minutes, give the hens a half of a turn (for nice grill marks) and continue to grill uncovered for 5 minutes longer.   Flip the hens and turn down the heat to medium.   Cover the grill and cook for five minutes.   Uncover the grill and continue cooking the hens, flipping them at 5 minute intervals for 10 to 15 minutes longer. Remove the hens from the grill and cover loosely with foil.   While the hens are resting, grill the orange slices until lightly browned.   Serve the grilled hens with the grilled orange slices and a sprinkling of the green onions.   Enjoy with a good dry Rose wine.

LIP SMACKING PIRI PIRI CHICKEN

Serves: 6 to 8

INGREDIENTS:

2 dried piri piri chiles or 2 dried chipotle chiles left whole

5 Jalapeno chiles stemmed, seeded, and chopped

2 tablespoons of fresh ginger grated

4 cloves of garlic chopped

2/3 cup packed cilantro leaves

2 tablespoons of apple cider vinegar

4 green onions sliced

½ cup of olive oil

1 teaspoon of salt and freshly cracked pepper

4 pounds of bone-in chicken pieces with skin on (preferably thighs)

Cooking spray

1/4 cup of parsley chopped as a garnish

DIRECTIONS:

In a food processor, puree the first 8 ingredients until smooth.   Season the puree with the salt and cracked pepper.   Reserve ½ cup of the puree as a dipping sauce if desired, but it is some hot stuff, baby! Not for every palate!!! Place the chicken pieces in a 9/13 baking dish and rub the remaining puree all over the chicken, coating them on both sides.   Marinate in the refrigerator for approximately 4 hours. The longer you marinate the chicken, the more flavor the meat will retain. Preheat oven to 450 degrees and turn on oven fan or your smoke alarms will certainly go off.   I learned that my Yellow Labrador does not like the smoke alarm!!   Place a couple of wire racks on a large rimmed cookie or baking sheet, covered with tin foil to save on clean up.   Shake the chicken pieces to remove some of the marinade and place the chicken on top of the wire rack on the prepared baking sheet.   Spray the chicken with the cooking spray.   Roast the chicken on the upper rack of the oven for 45 minutes until the chicken is cooked through.   Transfer chicken to a serving platter, sprinkle with the parsley and serve hot. This meal is delicious with your favorite rice, and a fresh green vegetable.   I like to serve it with a nice bottle of Pinot Noir, but my husband prefers a Heineken!   Dutchies!!

I LOVE PASTA CHICKEN ALFREDO

Serves: 4

INGREDIENTS:

1 ½ pounds of boneless chicken thighs (fat removed)

½ teaspoon of salt

Freshly cracked pepper

1/4 teaspoon of cayenne pepper

5 tablespoons of olive oil divided

8 ounces of fettuccine or Pappardelle pasta

1 red bell pepper sliced

8 ounces of crimini mushrooms quartered

1 bunch of asparagus (tough ends cut off) sliced into 2" pieces

2 carrots sliced on an angle 1/4" thick

3 green onions sliced on an angle

5 large garlic cloves sliced

1 ½ cups of chicken broth

3/4 cup of half and half

3 tablespoons of flour

1 ½ cups of grated parmigiano reggiano or romano cheese

½ cup of reserved pasta water (if needed)

DIRECTIONS:

Cut chicken into bite size generous pieces and place in a bowl. Toss the chicken with the salt, pepper and cayenne pepper. Heat 2 tablespoons of oil in a large skillet or wok (preferably) until hot but not smoking. Add the chicken and cook quickly on all sides until done. Remove the chicken from the pan and reserve. Cook the pasta according to package, but just until al dente, reserving ½ cup of pasta water. Please DO NOT rinse the pasta. Add the additional 3 tablespoons of oil to the skillet over medium high heat and add the bell pepper, mushrooms, asparagus and carrots. Stir fry until cooked through (about 6 to 7 minutes). Add the garlic and green onions and cook 2 minutes longer over medium heat. Combine the chicken broth, half and half and flour in a bowl and whisk until smooth. Add broth mixture and the chicken to the vegetables and bring to a boil until thickened.   If too thick, add some of the reserved pasta water.   Add the cheese and stir until incorporated. Add the pasta and toss.   Salt and pepper to taste and serve immediately.

SWEET & MOIST BARBEQUE CHICKEN THIGHS

Serves: 4

INGREDIENTS:

8 boneless skinless chicken thighs (fat removed)

1teaspoon of salt

1teaspoon of freshly cracked pepper

½ teaspoon of cayenne pepper

½ teaspoon of smoked paprika

4 teaspoons of canola oil

1 cup of barbeque sauce (preferably Sweet Baby Ray's)

DIRECTIONS:

Place chicken thighs in a 9 x 13 glass dish.   Mix together the salt, pepper, cayenne pepper and smoked paprika in a small dish.   Coat the chicken thighs with the canola oil and sprinkle all over with the spice mixture.   Heat a gas grill over high heat until it reaches 400 degrees. Place spiced chicken directly on the grill and cook with the grill open until nicely grill-marked on one side (about 5 minutes).   Using a metal spatula, flip chicken thighs and generously brush cooked side with the barbeque sauce.   Continue cooking another 5 minutes until grill-marked and flip the thighs again.   Brush with the barbeque sauce and cook 3 minutes longer. Continue brushing and flipping the thighs until nicely grill marked.

CHICKEN BREAST POCKETS WITH PROSCUITTO

Serves: 6

INGREDIENTS:

6 large boneless skinless chicken breasts

1 teaspoon of salt

1 teaspoon of pepper

1 teaspoon of paprika divided

6 slices of fresh mozzarella cheese sliced 1/4" thick

12 thin slices of proscuitto

½ cup of parsley chopped

2 tablespoon of olive oil

2 cups of chicken broth

1 bay leaf

1/4 teaspoon of thyme

4 tablespoons of butter

Freshly cracked pepper

Al Dente wide egg noodles, buttered

Poppy seeds

DIRECTIONS:

Preheat oven to 400 degrees.   With a kitchen mallet or hammer, flatten each chicken breast in a large sealable bag to a uniform thickness. Place the chicken breasts on a work surface and sprinkle with the salt, pepper, and ½ teaspoon of paprika.   Place one slice of mozzarella cheese in the center of each breast and top with two slices of the proscuitto.   Sprinkle the breasts liberally with the parsley.   Starting at one corner of each breast, pull the chicken meat up and over the filling and secure with toothpicks.   Flip the breasts over and brush with the olive oil and sprinkle with the remaining paprika.   Place breasts in a 9 x 13 glass dish. Add the chicken broth, bay leaf, thyme and butter to the glass dish.   Place chicken in the oven and cook for 15 minutes uncovered.   Baste the chicken with the chicken broth and continue to bake, basting occasionally with the broth, for about 15 minutes until the cheese is beginning to ooze out and the chicken is cooked.   Let the chicken breasts cool for 5 minutes.   Remove the toothpicks from the breasts.   Serve in large flat bowls over buttered wide egg noodles and tarragon green beans (see page 143).   Ladle a few tablespoons of the cooked broth over the entire dish and serve immediately.

LEMON & HERB ROASTED CHICKEN

Serves: 2 to 4

INGREDIENTS:

1 Five pound whole chicken, cleaned and patted dry

Kosher salt

Black pepper

2 lemons sliced into ½" thick rounds

8 cloves of garlic

5 sprigs of fresh thyme

4 tablespoons of butter, softened

2 teaspoons of fresh rosemary, chopped fine

3 teaspoons of fresh tarragon, chopped fine

DIRECTIONS:

Preheat oven to 425 degrees.   Generously salt and pepper the cavity of the chicken.   Place the chicken in a greased large roasting pan.   Stuff the cavity of the chicken with 2 slices of lemon, 2 garlic cloves and the thyme sprigs.   Mix the softened butter with the rosemary and tarragon.   Using your fingers, gently loosen the skin of the chicken breasts and thighs creating a pocket between the skin and the meat.   Stuff the pockets with three tablespoons of the herb butter distributing it as evenly as possible.   Rub the outside of the chicken with the remaining herb butter.   Generously salt and pepper the outside of the chicken.   Arrange the remaining lemon slices and garlic around the chicken.   Roast the chicken for 45 minutes and check for doneness.   Juices from the thigh meat should run clear when pierced with a fork, or use a meat thermometer to check for doneness.   Remove the chicken from the oven and let it rest 15 minutes before carving.

IRRESISTIBLE BRAISED DUCK LEGS

Serves: 4

INGREDIENTS:

4 whole duck legs from the butcher, excess fat removed

1 teaspoon of salt

1 teaspoon of freshly cracked pepper

½ teaspoon of sweet paprika

2 tablespoons of olive oil

½ cup of quality red Port

8 whole cloves of garlic

5 sprigs of fresh lemon thyme

3 cups of low sodium chicken stock

1 cup of water

1 cup of dried cherries or cranberries divided

DIRECTIONS:

Preheat oven to 375 degrees.   Season the duck legs with the salt, pepper and paprika.   In a Dutch oven, heat the olive oil over medium high heat until hot but not smoking.   Add the seasoned duck legs and cook on each side until nicely golden brown.   Remove the duck legs and pour off excess grease from the pan.   Return the pan to the stove top over medium heat and add the Port.   Cook the Port in the pan while scraping up the brown bits using a spatula until the Port has reduced by half.   Add the garlic and lemon thyme.   Return the duck to the Dutch oven and add the chicken stock and water.   Place the Dutch oven in the preheated oven for 2 hours uncovered.   Remove the duck from the Dutch oven and keep warm.   Degrease the cooking liquid once slightly cooled.   Using a strainer to collect the solids, pour the cooking liquid into a medium sauce pan.   Add the dried cherries to liquid in the sauce pan. Heat the cooking liquid to a boil and reduce by one-half.   Serve the warm duck legs with the sauce and roasted brussel sprouts.

CRISPY ROASTED WHOLE DUCK

Serves: 2 to 4

INGREDIENTS:

1 large store bought frozen duck defrosted

2 teaspoons of sea salt

1 teaspoon of pepper

½ cup of fresh sage sliced

1 orange quartered

DIRECTIONS:

Preheat the oven to 250 degrees.   Trim the duck of all excess fat.   Season duck inside and out with the salt and pepper.   Stuff the duck with the fresh sage and quartered orange. Prick the duck all over with a fork on both sides, about 30 times piercing the skin.   Place the duck on a rack set in a large roasting pan.   Roast the duck breast side up for one hour.   Prick the duck with a fork thoroughly on the breast side and flip the duck over on the rack.   Prick the back side all over with a fork and return to the oven and roast for another hour.   Repeat this process for two more hours, flipping the duck after an hour and pricking it all over with a fork.   After four and one half hours of cooking, increase the oven temperature to 375 degrees and continue cooking for 30 minutes or until you have a nice crispy skin.   Let the duck rest for 10 minutes.   Carve and serve.

VARKENSVLEES

Pork

PIQUANT PORK SCHNITZEL
WITH SAVORY MUSHROOM GRAVY

Serves: 2 to 3

INGREDIENTS:

6 pork cutlets 1/4" thick

1/4 cup of seasoned flour (salt, pepper, paprika)

1 beaten egg mixed with 1 tablespoon of water

1 cup of panko bread crumbs

3/4 cup of butter

lemon wedges optional (light alternative to serving Schnitzel with gravy)

4 tablespoons of olive oil

½ cup of chopped yellow onion

12 ounces of button mushrooms sliced

3 cloves of garlic minced

1/3 cup of flour

2 cups of beef stock

2 tablespoons of Sherry

1 tablespoon of chopped parsley

DIRECTIONS:

If making gravy, heat olive oil over medium high heat in a large sauce pan. Add onions and saute for about 5 minutes. Add the button mushrooms and continue to saute for another 5 minutes, turning the mushrooms until they are golden brown. Add the garlic and cook 1 minute longer. Add the flour to the mushroom pan and lower the heat to medium. Stir the mushrooms constantly for 1 minute. Slowly add the beef stock and stir until smooth. Increase the heat, add the Sherry and let sauce come to a boil until thickened. Turn off heat, stir in parsley and cover mushroom sauce. Cut tiny slits around the edges of the pork cutlets to keep them from curling while cooking. Season the flour with salt, pepper and paprika. Dip each pork cutlet in the flour mixture. Next, dip the cutlet in the egg and finally in the panko, pressing the panko into the pork. In a large skillet, melt the butter over medium heat. When melted and just sizzling, add the pork cutlets and cook for about 2 to 3 minutes per side until golden brown on both sides. Serve immediately with the gravy.   If making a light version, serve with lemon wedges and squeeze the lemon over the cutlets.

ASIAN-GLAZED GRILLED PORK TENDERLOIN

Serves: 4

INGREDIENTS:

½ cup of unseasoned rice wine vinegar

1/4 cup of low sodium soy sauce

1 tablespoons of brown sugar

1 tablespoon of sesame oil

1 ½ teaspoons of chile paste (such as Sambal Oelek)

8 cloves of garlic peeled and minced

1 pork tenderloin, silver skin removed

DIRECTIONS:

In a small bowl, whisk together the first six ingredients through the minced garlic. Pour mixture into a sealable bag and add the pork tenderloin. Marinate the tenderloin for two hours. Remove the pork from the bag. Heat a gas grill to 400 degrees and then uncover and oil the grates of the grill. Place tenderloin on an uncovered grill and cook on each side until nicely grill-marked, turning as necessary. The tenderloin should take approximately 20 minutes. Using a meat thermometer, check for doneness. Serve pork with brown rice and stir-fried vegetables.

FRANK LOVES PASTA CARBONARA

Serves: 4 to 6

INGREDIENTS:

1 pound of Bucatini pasta (spaghetti or linguine work well also)

3 eggs beaten

¾ pound of good quality pancetta cut into ¼ to ½" dice (or thick sliced bacon)

2 tablespoons of extra virgin olive oil

3 cups of finely grated parmigiano Reggiano cheese

2 tablespoons of finely chopped parsley

DIRECTIONS:

Fill a large pot with water, add salt (the water should taste like the sea) and bring to a rolling boil. Add the pasta and cook until the pasta is al dente. Do not overcook the pasta! While the pasta is cooking, add the olive oil to a large skillet and cook the pancetta until slightly browned. Remove the skillet from the heat and set aside. Drain the pasta reserving one cup of water. Add the pasta to the skillet with the pancetta. Place the beaten eggs in a bowl and slowly whisk in about a ¼ cup of the reserved pasta water. Add the cheese to the eggs mixture and mix to incorporate. Quickly add the egg mixture to the warm pasta and toss continuously to incorporate and cook the eggs.   If necessary, add more of the reserved pasta water to the desired creaminess.   Fold in the parsley and serve immediately.   That's Amore!

DELICIOSO CARNITAS

Serves: 8

INGREDIENTS:

5 pounds of boneless pork shoulder trimmed of excess fat

1 tablespoon of salt

Freshly cracked black pepper

1 tablespoon of smoked paprika

2 tablespoons of canola oil

2 cups of chicken stock

Water

2 cinnamon sticks

2 teaspoons of chile powder

3 bay leaves

5 cloves of garlic peeled and sliced

DIRECTIONS:

Heat oven to 350 degrees. Cut the pork shoulder into 5 or 6 equal sized chunks. Season chunks all over with the salt, pepper and paprika. Heat the canola oil in a Dutch oven over medium high heat until hot but not smoking. Add the half of the pork pieces to the hot oil and brown on all sides (this is a key step and should not be rushed). Repeat with remaining pork pieces. You may cook them all at once if your cooking vessel is large enough. If the pork pieces are touching each other, they will not brown adequately. Once the pork is browned, remove it from the pan and wipe out the excess grease from the pan. Pour the chicken stock into the pan over medium heat and scrape up all of the brown bits on the bottom of the pan. Add the pork back to the Dutch oven and add enough water so that the pork pieces are one half submerged in the cooking liquid. Add the next four ingredients. Place the Dutch oven in the preheated oven and cook uncovered for 3 ½ hours, occasionally turning the pork pieces. Remove the pork from the oven. Once the pork is cool enough to handle, shred the pork with two forks into large bite-sized chunks, removing any big chunks of fat. Return the pork to the Dutch oven and continue cooking in the oven until all liquid has evaporated and the pork is slightly crispy, about 20 minutes.   Serve with small flour tortillas, salsa, sour cream, cilantro, sliced onions and sliced cabbage.

FOURTH OF JULY
SOUTH CAROLINA STYLE PULLED PORK

Serves: About 20

INGREDIENTS:

1 eight pound bone-in pork shoulder

4 tablespoons of cocoa coffee rub (see page 40)

1 tablespoon of cumin

4 cups of applewood chips for smoking

Small metal (not teflon) pan for smoking chips (2 stacked disposable pans work fine)

2 cups of cider vinegar

½ cup of ketchup

1/4 cup of brown sugar

3 teaspoons of sea salt

1 tablespoon of chile sauce (such as sambal oelek)

2 teaspoons of freshly cracked pepper

DIRECTIONS:

Cut excess fat off the pork shoulder and discard.   In a small bowl, mix the cocoa coffee rub with the cumin.   Rub the pork all over with the spices.   Wrap the pork in plastic wrap and place in a Pyrex dish in the refrigerator for 24 hours.   Prior to grilling the pork, remove from refrigerator for 30 minutes.   Heat the grill on one side only (two burners on and the rest of the burners off) covered until 350 degrees. Place one cup of the wood chips in the metal pan and place over the lit burners. Grill the pork shoulder on indirect heat with the fat side up with the grill covered about 3 hours, checking on it and adding more smoking chips as the chips get charred and are no longer producing smoke. Meanwhile, make the sauce in a saucepan by adding the vinegar through the pepper.   Bring to a boil and then keep warm. The internal temperature of the pork should be 170 degrees on a meat thermometer when it is done. Remove the pork from the grill and cover loosely with foil.   Allow the pork to rest for about 30 minutes.   Remove any fat from the pork roast and shred the meat with two forks.   In a crock pot on low heat, add the pork and toss with warm vinegar sauce.   Decorate the house

for the arriving party guests.   When ready to eat, pile the pork on fresh hamburger buns and
enjoy!

COWBOY BABY BACK RIBS

Serves: 4 to 6

INGREDIENTS:

2 full racks of baby back ribs

4 tablespoons of coffee cocoa rub (see page 40)

2 tablespoons of packed brown sugar

2 to 3 cups of your favorite barbeque sauce (sweet or smoky)

Heavy duty aluminum foil

DIRECTIONS:

Preheat the oven to 300 degrees.   Mix the coffee cocoa rub with brown sugar.   To prepare the ribs, either remove tough membrane from the ribs, or cut slits in the membrane between each bone.   Rub each rack of ribs with 3 tablespoons of the coffee cocoa sugar rub.   Place one rack of ribs on a large sheet of aluminum foil, meaty side down.   Place another large sheet of aluminum foil on top of the ribs and roll or fold all of the edges of the foil to make a completely sealed package.   The package should be about an inch larger than the ribs. Repeat with the other rack of ribs.   Place both packages on a large rimmed baking sheet and place in the oven for 2 ½ hours.   Remove from the oven and light a gas grill to 400 degrees. Oil the grates of the grill and place the ribs on the grill, basting with generous amounts of barbeque saucing and turning as the ribs develop nice grill marks.   Serve immediately.

HERB BUTTER BONE-IN PORK CHOPS

Serves: 4

INGREDIENTS:

4 1" thick bone-in pork chops

4 tablespoons of olive oil (divided)

Kosher salt

Freshly cracked pepper

4 tablespoons of butter

2 large garlic cloves smashed

4 sprigs of fresh thyme

1 sprig of rosemary

DIRECTIONS:

Rub the pork chops all over with one tablespoon of olive oil. Generously sprinkle the chops with the kosher salt and cracked pepper. Heat the remaining olive oil in a large skillet over medium heat until hot but not smoking. Add the pork chops to the skillet and cook until nicely browned on one side, about 6 minutes. Turn the pork chops and continue cooking until browned, about 4 minutes. Add the butter to the skillet along with the garlic, thyme and rosemary. Cook the butter until it is browned, about a minute, and spoon over the pork chops. Serve with garlicky kale (see page 139) and sauteed mushrooms.

GRANDPA CARL'S SAUERKRAUT & KIELBASA

Serves: 8

INGREDIENTS:

2 large jars of sauerkraut

2 tablespoons of dehydrated onion flakes

1 cup of apple sauce

2 tablespoons of brown sugar

2 bay leaves

½ teaspoon of thyme

1 bottle of light beer

2 pounds of beef kielbasa or smoked sausage cut into 4" chunks

DIRECTIONS:

In a slow cooker, mix together all of the ingredients and cook on the low setting for 8 hours. Serve the sauerkraut and kielbasa with spaetzle (nifflees) - see page 147 and warm mashed potatoes.

VIS

Fish & Shellfish

PRESENTATION HALIBUT ASIAN-STYLE

Serves: 4

INGREDIENTS:

Parchment paper

4 six to seven ounce halibut fillets of equal thickness

4 heads of baby bok choy ends removed and sliced 1" thick

4 scallions sliced on the diagonal

1 red or orange bell pepper sliced into 1/8" strips

Zest from one orange (use a zester grater)

1 tablespoon of chopped cilantro

1 ½ teaspoons of toasted sesame seeds

2 teaspoons of freshly grated ginger (or ginger in the tube)

3 tablespoons of ponzu sauce (or low sodium soy sauce)

2 teaspoons of rice wine vinegar

1 teaspoon of Cholula sauce

1 teaspoon of sesame oil

DIRECTIONS:

Preheat oven to 400 degrees. Tear off four 20" sheets of parchment paper. Fold each sheet in half and cut out the shape of a half heart, using all 20" for the widest part of the half heart. Unfold the parchment paper and place a halibut fillet on one side of the heart. Repeat with remaining sheets of parchment. Top the halibut fillets with equal amount of the baby bok choy, scallions, bell pepper, zested orange peel, cilantro and toasted sesame seeds. Mix together the next five ingredients. Spoon an equal amount of sauce on top of each fillet. Fold the heart back into a half heart shape. Beginning at the top of the heart, begin making small folds (one on top of each other) all the way around to seal the fish completely with the parchment. You should end up with a round sealed packet. Secure the end fold with a paper clip if needed to keep it sealed. Place the packets on a rimmed baking sheet and place in the oven. Cook the fillets for 14 minutes. Transfer each packet to a serving plate.

SILKY SEARED SEA SCALLOPS
ON A BED OF BUTTERY SWEET CORN

Serves: 4

INGREDIENTS:

3 tablespoons of butter divided

4 ears of fresh yellow sweet corn shucked close to the ear

½ medium onion diced

1/2 cup of chicken broth

1 teaspoon of sea salt

1/4 cup of half and half

12 large sea scallops

½ teaspoon of Cayenne pepper

½ teaspoon of seasoned salt (such as Lawry's)

1 tablespoon of canola oil

4 tablespoons of butter divided

1/4 cup of chopped chives

DIRECTIONS:

In a large skillet, melt 2 tablespoons of the butter. When the butter is melted and sizzling, add the corn kernels, onion and salt and saute over medium heat for approximately 5 minutes until onion is translucent.   Add the chicken broth and deglaze the pan scraping up any bits on the bottom of the pan. Cook over medium low heat until the stock has reduced completely. Add the 2 tablespoon of butter and stir to melt. Add the half and half and keep warm. Dry the scallops with paper towel and season the scallops with the cayenne and seasoned salt. Heat the oil in a large skillet until just beginning to smoke over medium heat. Add the scallops flat side down. Let the scallops brown on one side undisturbed in the pan. You want a nice golden crust on each scallop which takes about one to two minutes depending on your stove top. When the scallops have formed a nice golden crust, flip them, add two tablespoons of butter to the pan and cook for one minute longer. Arrange a pile of the sweet corn on 4 plates and top with 3 scallops each. Sprinkle with the chives and serve immediately.

ROCKIN' ROCKEFELLER GRILLED OYSTERS

Serves: 6 as a hearty first course

INGREDIENTS:

12 Blue Point or large Alaskan oysters

1 tablespoons of unsalted butter

1 shallot finely chopped

1 green onion finely chopped

½ rib of celery finely chopped

1 clove of garlic minced

1 cup of spinach packed

1/4 cup of half and half

1/4 cup finely shredded gruyere cheese

2 tablespoons of panko

Lemon wedges

DIRECTIONS:

Heat the butter in a medium skillet over medium heat until melted.   Add the shallot, green onion and celery and saute 5 minutes until translucent.   Add the garlic and spinach and saute stirring constantly, about 1 minute.   Lower the heat to medium low and add the half and half and cook stirring for 3 minutes.   Remove from heat.   Mix the cheese with the panko crumbs. Heat a grill to 400 degrees.   Shuck the oysters retaining the juice.   Place the oysters on a baking sheet.   Top an equal amount of the spinach mixture on each shucked oyster.   Mix the cheese with the panko and sprinkle equal amounts of the mixture on top of the spinach mixture.   Place the baking sheet of oysters on the grill and cover for 5 minutes.   When the oysters are bubbling and starting to lightly brown, remove and serve with the lemon wedges.

COCONUT BASIL MUSSELS ON RICE

Serves: 2

INGREDIENTS:

2 pounds of fresh de-bearded mussels

2 cups of cooked Jasmine or white rice

1 14 ounce can of lite coconut milk

1/4 cup of white wine

½ cup of fresh basil leaves chopped

2 tablespoons of fish sauce (Asian aisle at grocery store)

1 lime juiced (zest the lime before juicing and reserve)

1 tablespoon of ponzu sauce

1 ½ teaspoons of chile sauce (such as Sambal Oelek)

1 tablespoon of olive oil

½ cup of red bell pepper chopped

2 shallots chopped

1 tablespoon of finely grated fresh ginger

4 cloves of garlic minced

Zest of one lime

1/2 cup of chicken broth

DIRECTIONS:

Prepare the rice and keep warm.   In a blender, add the coconut milk, white wine, basil leaves, fish sauce, lime juice, ponzu sauce and chile sauce and blend until incorporated.   Add the olive oil to a wok or large skillet and heat over medium high heat.   Add the red bell pepper, shallots, ginger, garlic and lime zest and saute 3 minutes.   Add the chicken broth and mussels to the pan and bring to a boil.   Cover the mussels and steam for 4 minutes. Uncover the pan, and if all mussels have just started to open, stir in the blender sauce, cover and simmer over medium low heat for 2 minutes until the sauce is heated through.   Serve the mussels and sauce over rice.

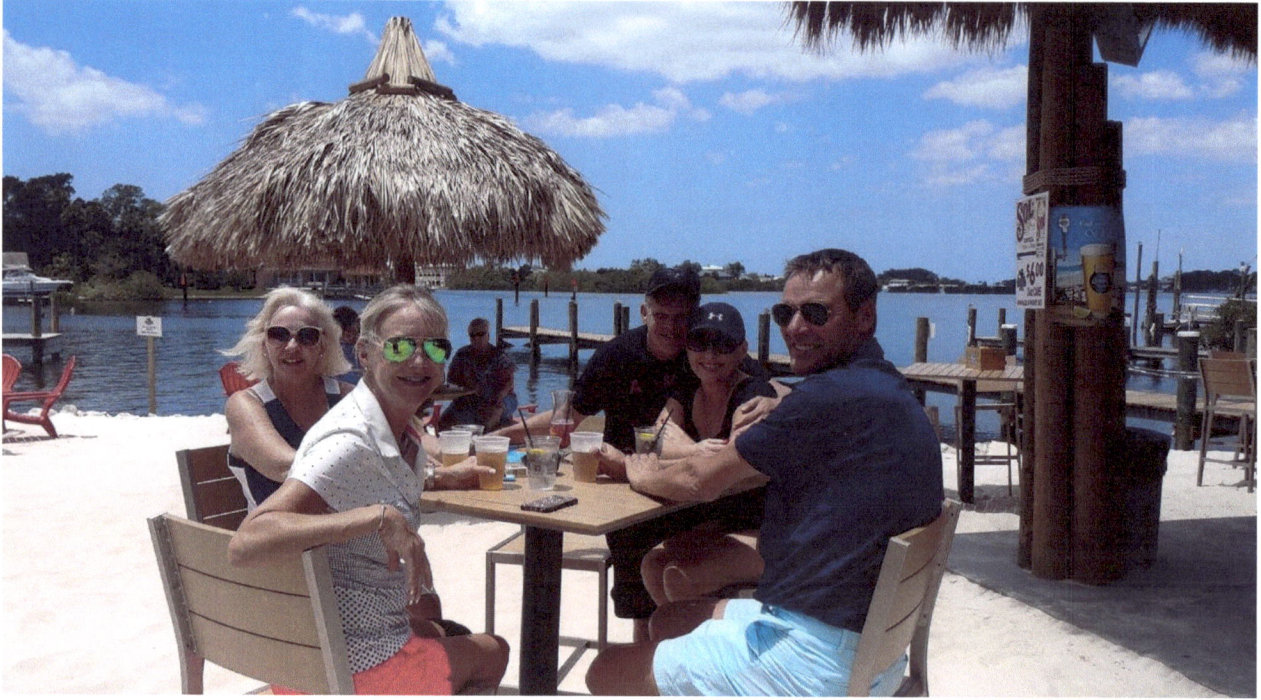

CURRIED TUNA SALAD ON CROISSANTS

Serves: 4

INGREDIENTS:

2 cans of all white meat tuna packed in water and drained

1/4 cup of slivered almonds

1/4 teaspoon of curry powder

1 tablespoon of finely chopped tarragon

2 tablespoons of capers

1 tablespoon of red onion minced

½ cup of good mayonnaise

1 tablespoon of whole-grain mustard

½ teaspoon of fine sea salt

½ teaspoon of freshly cracked pepper

Bibb Lettuce

4 croissants split

Green grapes as a garnish

DIRECTIONS:

In a medium size bowl, combine all of the ingredients through the black pepper and mix until well incorporated and the tuna is broken up.   Divide the tuna mixture equally on each of the split croissants and top with a couple of pieces of bib lettuce.   Top with the croissant halves and serve with a bunch of green grapes on the side.

CROWD PLEASING SAFFRON MUSSELS

Serves: 6 as an appetizer

INGREDIENTS:

3 pounds of fresh mussels de-bearded

½ cup of unsalted butter

1 teaspoon of sea salt

1 cup of red onion finely chopped

1 ½ tablespoons of fresh thyme chopped

6 cloves of garlic minced

2 cups of quality white wine

2 tablespoons of dijon mustard

1 tablespoon of chile sauce (such as Sambal Oelek)

½ teaspoon of saffron threads

½ cup of half and half

½ cup of green onions sliced thin on the diagonal

Fresh crusty french bread

DIRECTIONS:

Melt the butter in a large sauce pan over medium high heat.   Add the salt, onion, and thyme. Saute for 5 minutes until the onion is translucent.   Add the garlic and saute 1 minute longer. Add the white wine, dijon mustard, chile sauce and saffron threads.   Cook on the stove over medium high heat for 5 minutes until the saffron threads have melted into the broth and the broth is boiling.   Add the mussels to the sauce pan along with the half and half.   Cover the sauce pan and steam the mussels over medium heat for about 6 minutes.   When the mussels are open, take off the stove and ladle into 6 bowls with the sauce, and sprinkle each bowl with the thinly sliced green onions.   Serve with crusty bread for soaking up the sauce.

LOBSTA ROLLS & FRITTERS
'CUZ NO GOOD COOKBOOK CAN BE WITHOUT LOBSTA!

Serves: 8

INGREDIENTS:

1 cup of quality mayonnaise

1 tablespoon of whole grain mustard

1 tablespoon of olive oil

½ teaspoon of salt

½ teaspoon of freshly cracked pepper

1 tablespoon of fresh tarragon chopped

2 ribs of celery chopped fine

1 lemon juiced

1 ½ pounds of Maine lobster chopped into bite sized pieces

Fresh baked hot dog buns from the bakery

Fritters (see page 134)

DIRECTIONS:

Combine the all of the ingredients except the lobster in a bowl and whisk until smooth.   Add the lobster and stir to incorporate.   Pile the fresh buns with the lobster salad and serve with piping hot fritters.   Go to the Beach!

SOEPEN

Soups

A TASTE OF THAI CURRY SOUP

Serves: 4

INGREDIENTS:

2 cups of cooked white rice

3 tablespoons of olive oil

½ medium sweet onion sliced thin

1 ½ cups of sliced mushrooms

1 3" piece of ginger minced

2 garlic cloves minced

2 tablespoons of lemon grass in a tube (produce section)

2 teaspoons of red curry paste

1 quart of reduced sodium chicken stock

2 tablespoons of Ponzu or soy sauce

2 teaspoons of Agave nectar

2 cups of cooked shredded chicken (preferably thigh meat)

2 cups of chopped kale

1 can of light coconut milk

2 limes

Chopped cilantro

3 green onions sliced thin

DIRECTIONS:

Heat the olive oil in a large saucepan over medium heat.   Add the onions and mushrooms and cook until the onions are transparent.   Add the ginger, garlic cloves, lemon grass and red curry paste and cook until fragrant, about 1 minute.   Add a cup of the chicken stock and stir until the curry paste is dissolved.   Add the remaining stock, soy sauce and Agave Nectar. Bring the mixture to a boil and then reduce heat to a simmer and cook for 20 minutes covered. Stir in the kale and cooked chicken and bring back to a simmer for approximately 5 minutes. Add the coconut milk and the juice of one lime (my husband does not like lime juice, so you may omit this step if lime is not your favorite. Serve in bowls over cooked white rice and garnish with cilantro, green onions and lime wedges if desired.

FRANK'S CHINESE MEATBALL SOUP

Serves: 4

INGREDIENTS:

7 ounces of Enoki mushrooms

2 tablespoons of olive oil

1 tablespoon of balsamic vinegar

1 tablespoon of rice wine vinegar

3 tablespoons of water

½ pound of boneless skinless chicken thighs, fat removed and diced

½ pound of ground pork sausage

6 scallions sliced on the diagonal

1 tablespoon of freshly grated ginger

2 1-inch pieces of ginger peeled and sliced into thin matchstick pieces

½ teaspoon of cayenne pepper

1 teaspoon of salt

1 teaspoon of pepper

6 cups of unsalted chicken stock

1 can of drained bamboo shoots or sliced water chestnuts

2 large eggs beaten

2 teaspoons of sesame oil

1 tablespoon of Siracha sauce

DIRECTIONS:

In a saute pan, add the olive oil and saute the mushrooms until golden brown and set aside. In a small dish, mix the vinegars with the water and set aside. In a food processor, add the diced uncooked chicken, one tablespoon of the vinegar mixture, one-third of the sliced scallions, the grated ginger, cayenne pepper, salt and the pepper and pulse until incorporated and the chicken is ground. Remove mixture from food processor into a medium size bowl. Mix the pork into the chicken mixture until well incorporated and roll into approximately 20 one inch balls. Set aside. In a large soup pot, add the stock and ginger and bring to a gentle boil over medium high heat. Reduce heat, add the bamboo shoots, and let the stock simmer for 10 minutes.   Increase the heat to medium high and stir in the beaten eggs. Add the meatballs and mushrooms and simmer for 5 minutes.   Remove the pot from the stove and add the remaining vinegar mixture, sesame oil and Siracha sauce.   Ladle into four large soup bowls and garnish with additional scallions.

FINGER LICKING FRENCH ONION SOUP
BUT THE FRENCH WOULDN'T LICK THEIR FINGERS
IT'S CULTURAL

Serves: 6 as a hearty first course or 2 as a meal

INGREDIENTS:

6 tablespoons of unsalted butter

2 medium sweet onions sliced thin

1 tablespoon of fresh thyme chopped

½ teaspoon of sea salt

3/4 cup of quality drinking sherry

3 teaspoons of flour

2 bay leaves

32 ounces of low sodium beef broth

1 tablespoon of worcestershire

1 tablespoon of ketchup

1 cup of water

Freshly cracked pepper

2 baguette slices cut ½ inch thick

2 slices of gruyere cheese cut 1/8" thick, large enough to cover 6 ramekins or 2 oven-proof
        soup crocks

DIRECTIONS:

In a Dutch oven or large sauce pan, melt the butter over medium high heat until sizzling.   Add the sliced onions, thyme and salt and saute stirring for about 30 minutes until the onions are golden brown and carmelized. Lower heat to medium. Carefully add the sherry and stir until the sherry is completely reduced.   Lower the heat to medium low and stir in the flour.   Cook stirring for 1 minute.   Add the bay leaves and slowly add the beef broth stirring constantly. Add the worcestershire, ketchup and water and bring to a boil over medium high heat stirring to incorporate the ketchup.   Add a generous amount of freshly cracked pepper.   Reduce soup to a simmer and let cook for 10 minutes. Remove the bay leaves. Ladle the soup into 6 ramekins or 2 soup crocks.   Preheat oven to broil. Place a piece of sliced baguette on each crock and cover with the cheese slices.   Broil the soup crocks about 5" from the heat source for about 2 minutes until the cheese is golden brown.

SAUSAGE & LENTIL MINESTRONE SOUP

Serves: 8

INGREDIENTS:

1 pound of Italian sweet sausage

2 tablespoons of olive oil

1 cup of sweet onion chopped

2 cups of carrot chopped into ½" pieces

2 cups of celery sliced into ½" pieces

5 cloves of garlic minced

6 cups of low sodium beef broth

2 14-ounce cans of chopped fire-roasted tomatoes

2 bay leaves

1 ½   teaspoons of oregano

1 package of Truvia or Stevia sweetener

½ cup of lentils, sorted and washed

1 teaspoon of salt

Freshly cracked pepper

3 cups of chopped kale

3 tablespoons of parsley chopped

Grated parmigiano reggiano cheese

DIRECTIONS:

In a large soup pot or Dutch oven, cook the Italian sausage until nicely browned, remove from the pot, drain and set aside.   In the same pot, heat the olive oil over medium high heat and add the onion, carrot and celery.   Saute the vegetables until they are crisp tender.   Add the garlic to the pot and saute, stirring, for 1 to 2 minutes until fragrant. Add the beef broth, undrained fire-roasted tomatoes, bay leaves, oregano, sweetener and lentils.   Bring soup pot to a boil and then reduce heat to a simmer. Taste the soup and adjust seasonings with salt and pepper if needed. Cover the pot and continue cooking the soup for 50 minutes, or until the lentils are tender.   Add the kale and cook for another 5 minutes.   Stir in the parsley and serve the soup with freshly grated parmigiano reggiano cheese and crusty bread.

BABY IT'S COLD OUTSIDE
VIETNAMESE PHO

Serves: 4 to 6

INGREDIENTS:

2 medium yellow onions quartered

5" piece of ginger halved lengthwise

4 pounds of low sodium beef stock

2 cinnamon sticks

5 cardamom pods

5 whole star anise

4 cloves

1 tablespoon of fennel seeds

1 tablespoon of coriander seeds

1/4 cup of fish sauce

2 teaspoons of agave Nectar or Stevia

2 pounds of ribeye steak, fat removed, sliced as thin as possible

Cooked rice noodles

Fresh cilantro, mint and basil

Lime wedges

Bean sprouts

Thinly sliced jalapeno pepper (optional)

DIRECTIONS:

Place the yellow onions and ginger halves on a baking sheet and broil in the oven until nicely charred. Pour the beef stock in a soup pot. Add the charred vegetables. Place the cinnamon sticks, cardamom pods, anise, cloves, fennel seeds and coriander in a piece of cheesecloth and tie off the end making a bundle. Add the cheesecloth spice bundle to the beef stock and add the agave nectar and fish sauce. Bring the stock to a boil and reduce the heat to a simmer. Simmer the stock for 1 ½ hours partially covered. Remove the charred vegetables and cheesecloth bundle from the pot. Add the sliced beef and return to a simmer until the meat is just cooked through. Add the cooked noodles. Serve the Pho in large bowls and garnish with the herbs, lime juice, bean sprouts and sliced jalapeno (if desired).

Marrying the man of my dreams·······..

BIJGERECHTEN

Side Dishes

SAVORY & LIGHT POTATO GRATIN

Serves: 12

INGREDIENTS:

3 tablespoons of olive oil (divided)

3 large cloves of garlic sliced

1 large sweet onion chopped

2 teaspoons of fresh thyme chopped

1 teaspoon of sea salt

4 large russet potatoes sliced thin on a mandolin

Freshly cracked pepper

1 cup of gruyere cheese grated

4 tablespoons of capers drained

1 14 ounce can of vegetable or chicken broth

DIRECTIONS:

Grease a 9 x 13" glass casserole dish with 1 tablespoon of the olive oil. Sprinkle slice garlic cloves over the oil. In a large skillet heat the remaining 2 tablespoons of oil over medium heat. Add the onions, thyme and salt and saute stirring occasionally until onions are translucent and beginning to turn golden brown, about 15 minutes. Preheat oven to 325 degrees. Layer one-third of the potatoes over the sliced garlic. Sprinkle with freshly cracked pepper, half of the cooked onion mixture, 1/3 cup of grated cheese, and a third of the capers. Repeat layer. Spread remaining potato slices over the gratin and pour the can of chicken broth over the gratin. Press the gratin down with your hands to compact and distribute the broth. Cover with the remaining capers. Cover the gratin with tin foil and place in the preheated oven for 1 ½ hours. Remove gratin from the oven and carefully uncover. Add the remaining cheese to the top of the gratin and return to the oven. Bake the gratin another 15 to 20 minutes until the cheese is melted and golden brown. Let the gratin sit for 10 minutes, cut into squares and serve.

GRANDMA DORIS' POTATO FRITTERS

Serves: 4

INGREDIENTS:

2 pounds Russet potatoes peeled and sliced 1/8" thick lengthwise

1 ½ cups of flour

1 cup of water

1 teaspoon of Lawry's seasoned salt

Canola oil

DIRECTIONS:

In a medium bowl, whisk the flour with the water and salt until smooth.   Pour enough canola oil in a Dutch oven or large sauce pan so that it is approximately 5 inches deep and heat over medium high heat.   Once the oil is hot enough to fry (you can test it by dripping a small amount of the batter in the pan; if it sizzles and floats to the top, your oil is hot enough).   Dip the potato slices in the batter, letting the batter drip off, and fry the fritters in the oil in batches until golden brown.   Drain the cooked fritters on a wire rack or paper towels.   Add more salt if needed and serve the fritters hot.

SPICED SAUTEED BABY BOK CHOY

Serves: 4

INGREDIENTS:

2 tablespoons of canola oil

1 shallot sliced thin

3 cloves of garlic minced

2 tablespoons of freshly grated ginger or ginger in the tube

1 teaspoon of chile paste (such as Sambal Oelek)

4 bunches of baby bok choy, ends trimmed, halved lengthwise

3 tablespoons of ponzu sauce

1/4 teaspoon of sesame oil

2 scallions thinly sliced on the diagonal

DIRECTIONS:

Heat the canola oil in a wok or large skillet over medium high heat until hot but not smoking. Add the shallot and stir fry for 3 minutes. Add the garlic, ginger and chile paste and stir fry for 1 minute. Reduce the heat to medium and add the halved baby bok choy and cook 3 minutes longer, turning the bok choy. Add the ponzu sauce, sesame oil and scallions and cover the pan. Cook for 2 minutes. Uncover the pan and cook until all of the liquid is evaporated and the bok choy is fork tender. Serve.

INDULGENT SWEET CORN PUDDING SOUFFLE

Serves: 6 to 8

INGREDIENTS:

8 ears of sweet corn

1 can of sweetened condensed milk

4 eggs

1 stick of salted butter melted

Freshly cracked pepper

DIRECTIONS:

Preheat oven to 350 degrees. In a large pot, boil the sweet corn until just tender. Remove the corn from the pot and place in a cold water bath to cool and stop the cooking process. Cut the kernels from each corn cob and discard the cobs. In a blender or food processor, blend the corn, condensed milk, eggs, butter and freshly cracked pepper until smooth. Pour the mixture in a greased 2 quart casserole dish. Bake at 350 degrees for one hour until golden brown. Watch your guests gobble it up.

GARDEN FRESH SPICY YELLOW SQUASH

Serves: 4

INGREDIENTS:

1 tablespoon of sesame oil

1 tablespoon of canola oil

4 yellow squash cut into 1/4" wide strips, 3 inches long

3 garlic cloves sliced thin

1/4 cup of ponzu sauce

2 tablespoons of chile paste (such as Sambal Oelek)

2 teaspoons of agave nectar

2 tablespoons of toasted sesame seeds

DIRECTIONS:

Heat the sesame oil and canola oil in a large skillet over medium high heat until hot but not smoking. Add the squash strips and stir fry for 4 minutes. Add the garlic and stir fry one minute longer over medium heat. Whisk the ponzu sauce, chile paste and agave nectar in a small bowl and add to the skillet. Toss the squash and sprinkle with the toasted sesame seeds. Declicious with any Asian meal!

FRAT PARTY BAKED BEANS
(UNLIKELY TO BE FOUND ON A HEART-SMART MENU)

Serves: 6

INGREDIENTS:

1 tablespoon of olive oil

1 shallot chopped

1 pound of lean ground beef (90/10 beef to fat ratio)

1 teaspoon of worcestershire sauce

1/3 cup of brown sugar

1 cup of ketchup

1 tablespoon of whole-grain mustard

1 package of Lipton's onion soup mix

2 one pound cans of bacon-flavor baked beans

DIRECTIONS:

Preheat the oven to 350 degrees.   In a medium skillet heat the oil until hot but not smoking over medium high heat.   Add the shallot and saute until shallot is translucent, about 4 minutes.   Add the ground beef, breaking it up, and brown on all sides.   Drain the ground beef mixture and place in a large mixing bowl.   Add the worcestershire sauce, brown sugar, ketchup, mustard, soup mix and baked beans.   Mix thoroughly to incorporate all ingredients. Pour the mixture into a square casserole dish and bake uncovered in the oven for 50 minutes until bubbly.   Cool casserole for 10 minutes and serve.

GARLICKY KALE

Serves: 4

INGREDIENTS:

3 tablespoons of olive oil

1/3 cup of sweet onion chopped

3 cloves of garlic sliced thin

1 bunch of kale, tough stems removed, chopped

½ cup of chicken broth

DIRECTIONS:

In a large skillet, heat the olive oil over medium high heat.   Add the onion and cook until the onion is translucent.   Add the garlic and cook until fragrant, about 30 seconds.   Add the kale and stir fry until the kale is coated in the oil and starting to turn bright green.   Add the chicken broth to the skillet and reduce the heat to medium.   Simmer the kale until cooked through, about 5 minutes, and serve.

PANCETTA ROASTED BRUSSEL SPROUTS

Serves: 8

INGREDIENTS:

2 tablespoons of olive oil divided

2 pounds of brussel sprouts, ends removed and halved lengthwise

3 garlic cloves minced

1 tablespoon of shallot minced

½ pound of pancetta diced into 1/4" cubes

Freshly cracked pepper

DIRECTIONS:

Preheat oven to 450 degrees.   Brush a 9 x 13 glass casserole dish with 1 tablespoon of the olive oil. In a large mixing bowl, mix the brussel sprouts with the remaining tablespoon of oil, garlic, shallot, pancetta, and freshly cracked pepper.   Pour the brussel sprout mixture into the greased casserole dish.   Place the casserole dish in the oven and roast for 12 minutes. Stir the sprouts and continue roasting for an additional 10 minutes until the sprouts are fork tender.

TARRAGON GREEN BEANS & RED BELL PEPPERS

Serves: 8

INGREDIENTS:

2 pounds of fresh green beans, stem ends trimmed

3 tablespoons of olive oil

6 garlic cloves chopped

1 tablespoon of fresh tarragon chopped

1 teaspoon of fresh thyme chopped

1 large red bell pepper cut into 1/4" slices lengthwise

½ teaspoon of sea salt

Freshly cracked pepper

2 tablespoons of butter

DIRECTIONS:

Cook the beans in a pot of boiling water until crisp tender, about 2 minutes. Drain and rinse the beans with cold water to stop the cooking process. Let the beans dry. In a large skillet or work, heat the olive oil over medium heat. Add the garlic, tarragon and thyme and cook until the garlic is fragrant but not browned. Add the green beans, salt and red bell pepper and stir fry for about 6 minutes until the beans and peppers are cooked through, but still slightly crisp. Add cracked pepper and the butter and cook one minute longer. Serve immediately.

SAUTEED BALSAMIC MUSHROOMS

Serves: 4

INGREDIENTS:

2 tablespoons of olive oil

1 shallot chopped

1 teaspoon of sea salt

24 ounces of Crimini mushrooms wiped cleaned, quartered

4 tablespoons of unsalted butter

3 cloves of garlic minced

1/4 cup of quality dry red wine

2 tablespoons of quality balsamic vinegar

DIRECTIONS:

In a large skillet over medium high heat, heat the olive oil until hot but not smoking. Add the shallot and salt and saute for 2 minutes, or until the shallots are translucent (turn the heat down if they begin to burn). Add the quartered Crimini mushrooms and cook until nicely golden on all sides. Add the butter and the garlic cloves and stir into the mushrooms until fragrant, about one minute. Add the red wine and reduce completely. Add the balsamic vinegar and stir to coat the mushrooms. Serve immediately.

MOM'S GERMAN SPAETZLE
(NIFFLEES)

Serves: 6

INGREDIENTS:

4 eggs

1 cup plus 2 tablespoons of flour

1 teaspoon of salt

3 tablespoons of butter melted

1 tablespoon chives finely chopped

DIRECTIONS:

In a medium bowl, whisk the eggs until smooth. Add the flour and salt to the eggs and mix thoroughly until the batter is smooth. Mix the chives into the batter. Heat a large pan of salted water and bring to a boil. Dip a spoon into the boiling water. Using the edge of the spoon, spoon a small amount of batter from your batter bowl and dip spoon in the boiling water to release the nifflee. The amount of batter you use per nifflee should be about a teaspoon. Working quickly continue adding nifflees to the boiling water and boil until the nifflees float to the top. Remove the first batch of nifflees to a colander and repeat until all of the batter is used. Melt the butter in a large sauce pan over medium heat and fry the nifflees in the butter for about 3 minutes. Serve the nifflees with sauerkraut and keilbasa.

AUNT BARB'S GERMAN POTATO SALAD

Serves: 4

INGREDIENTS:

4 Russet potatoes with skins on, washed

3 slices of fried bacon crumbled

3/4 cup low sodium chicken broth, heated until hot

½ cup thinly sliced green onion

½ cup apple cider vinegar

2 tablespoons canola oil

1 teaspoon of salt

1 teaspoon of freshly cracked pepper

DIRECTIONS:

In a large pot of water, boil the potatoes until fork tender. Remove the potatoes from the water and let cool enough to handle the potatoes. Peel the potatoes, slice them into 1/8" rounds and place in a serving bowl with the crumbled bacon and sliced green onions. Mix the cider vinegar with canola oil, salt and pepper. Pour the cider mixture and the hot broth over the potatoes and mix to incorporate, trying not to break up the potatoes. Let the potatoes stand at room temperature for a half hour and mix again before serving.

BRUNCH

Brunch

A TASTE OF GERMANY POTATO PANCAKES

Serves: 6

INGREDIENTS:

4 large russet potatoes

2 eggs beaten

2 tablespoons of flour

½ teaspoon of salt

½ teaspoon of pepper

1/4 cup of grated sweet onion

Canola oil for frying

DIRECTIONS:

Peel and grate the potatoes and drain well in a colander. In a large mixing bowl, mix the eggs with the flour, salt and pepper until smooth. Add the potatoes and onion to the egg mixture and mix thoroughly until incorporated. In a large heavy skillet, heat enough oil to cover the bottom with an 1/8" depth. When the oil is hot, drop the potato mixture by large spoonfuls into the oil and flatten. Fry the pancakes about 2 to 3 minutes per side, in batches, until golden brown. Drain on paper towels and serve hot with applesauce and maple syrup.

Janie May

Sping, Spang, Sputter,
SPLOT!

JANIE'S CROQUE MADAMES

Serves: 2

INGREDIENTS:

1" thick slices of fresh sourdough bread

2 tablespoons of sour cream

1 clove of garlic minced

½ teaspoon of Dijon mustard

Salt and pepper to taste

2 slices of ham off the bone cut 1/4" thick

3/4 cup of Gruyere cheese grated

1 tablespoon of butter

2 large eggs

DIRECTIONS:

Heat the oven broiler. On a sheet pan, lightly broil the bread until dry but not browned. In a small bowl, mix the sour cream, garlic and mustard. Spread each bread slice with a scant amount of the sour cream mixture. Lay a ham slice on each bread slice and top each with half of the remaining sour cream mixture. Over the ham, divide the grated cheese between each sandwich, using it all. Heat the butter in a medium skillet and fry the eggs to your preference (but no more than over easy). While the eggs are cooking, place the sandwiches under the broiler and broil until the cheese is bubbly and golden. Top each sandwich with a fried egg and serve immediately.

BRUNCH FOR A CROWD
CRISPY HAM & EGG "MUFFINS"

Serves: 6 to 8

INGREDIENTS:

Olive oil cooking spray

12 slices of good quality ham, sliced fairly thin, from the deli

12 large eggs

Salt and Pepper

½ cup of diced Gouda (1/4" cubes)

½ cup of chives minced

DIRECTIONS:

Preheat oven to 400 degrees. Spray a 12 muffin baking tin with a light coating of olive oil cooking spray. Nestle a slice of ham in each muffin cup so that a small amount of ham is hanging over the edge of each cup. Crack an egg into each muffin cup and sprinkle with salt and pepper. Arrange equal amount of the Gouda pieces on top of each egg yolk. Bake the ham and egg muffins for approximately 15 minutes, until the whites are set and the yolks are still runny. Remove from oven and place an egg or two on each plate and sprinkle with the minced chives. Serve with country potatoes, sourdough toast and fresh fruit. These are super tasty and easy to prepare!

TOMORROW'S EGG CASSEROLE

Serves: 10 to 12

INGREDIENTS:

12 ounces of mild Italian sausage

10 eggs

2 cups of milk

4 untoasted English muffins cut into 1" cubes

1 cup of grated Gouda cheese

½ cup of diced red onion

½ cup of diced red pepper

Salt and pepper

DIRECTIONS:

Fry the Italian sausage in a skillet until cooked through. In a large bowl, whisk the eggs with the milk until the eggs are incorporated. Mix in the English muffin cubes, grated Gouda, green onion and red pepper. Pour the mixture in a greased 9 by 13 glass baking dish. Cover the dish with plastic wrap and refrigerate overnight. Remove the dish from the refrigerator and let it sit at room temperature for approximately 15 minutes. In a preheated 350 degree oven, bake the casserole for approximately 40 minutes until nicely golden and cooked through. Serve with fresh fruit, and country potatoes.

NAGERECHT

Dessert

ISIE'S LEMON FINGERS

Serves: A crowd

INGREDIENTS:

2 cups sifted flour

3/4 cup of melted butter

2 cups of sugar

3 eggs

6 tablespoons of fresh lemon juice

4 tablespoons of flour

½ cup of Confectioner's sugar

DIRECTIONS:

Preheat the oven to 350 degrees. Mix the flour and melted butter thoroughly until incorporated. Press the flour and butter mixture in an even layer in a 9 x 13 glass baking dish. Bake in the preheated oven for 15 minutes and remove from oven. In a large mixing bowl, mix the sugar, eggs, lemon juice and flour until well incorporated. Pour the mixture over the crust and return the pan to the oven. Bake for 25 minutes. Remove the pan from the oven and let cool for 15 minutes. Sprinkle with the confectioner's sugar and cut into even squares in the pan while warm.

CANDY BAR DELIGHT

Serves: A crowd

INGREDIENTS:

1 ½ cup of heavy whipping cream

3 tablespoons of sugar

1 teaspoon of vanilla

2 packages of soft lady fingers

1 16 ounce package of crunchy candy bars such as Heath or Butterfingers

     (Crushed into 1/4" bits with a hammer or heavy mallet)

1 cup of chopped pecans

DIRECTIONS:

In a large mixing bowl, using a whisk or blender, mix together the whipping cream, sugar and vanilla until thickened and high peaks form.   In a 9 x 13 glass baking dish, layer the bottom with 1 package of the lady fingers.   Spread one half of the whipped cream on top of the lady fingers and sprinkle with one half of the crushed candy bars.   Repeat process with a layer of lady fingers, whipped cream, crushed candy bars and top with the chopped pecans.   Chill the dessert in the refrigerator until ready to serve.   Cut the dessert into squares and enjoy!

PETER'S APPLE PIE

Serves: 8

INGREDIENTS:

1 store-bought pie crust, partially thawed

4 Granny Smith apples, sliced

1 tart red skinned apple, sliced

1 cup of shredded cheddar cheese

2 tablespoons of Wondra flour

1 ½ cups of organic sugar (divided)

1 stick of butter, melted (divided)

1 cup of whole wheat flour

1/4 teaspoon of almond extract

½ teaspoon of vanilla

DIRECTIONS:

Preheat oven to 350 degrees.   Place the partially thawed pie crust in a oven proof pie plate and cut a couple of small slits in the crust.   In a large bowl, mix together the apples, cheddar cheese, Wondra flour, ½ cup of the organic sugar, and half of the melted butter.   Pour mixture over the pie crust and press it down to fill any gaps. Add the almond extract and vanilla to the remaining melted butter and mix well.   To make the pie topping, mix together the remaining sugar and whole wheat flour.   Add the melted butter, almond extract and vanilla mixture to the dry ingredients and mix vigorously with a fork until the topping is a crumb-like texture. Pour the topping over the apples and gently press it to the edges of the pie, leaving the crumbled texture.   Bake the pie with a pan underneath to catch any seepage for about one hour.   Your house will smell amazing!

INDEX

Tomorrow's Egg Casserole, 154

Brussel Sprouts

Pancetta Roasted Brussel Sprouts, 140

Cabbage

Ginger Sesame Asian Slaw , 30

Chicken

BBQ Spatchcock Cornish Game Hens, 75

Chicken Breast Pockets with Proscuitto, 83

Citrus Ginger Chicken Noodle Salad, 71

Greek Salad with Blackened Chicken, 28

Happy Belly Chicken Pot Pie, 73

I Love Pasta Chicken Alfredo, 79

Lemon & Herb Roasted Chicken, 85

Lip Smacking Piri Piri Chicken, 77

Sweet & Moist Barbeque Chicken Thighs, 81

Corn

Indulgent Sweet Corn Pudding Souffle, 136

Silky Seared Sea Scallops on a Bed of Buttery Sweet Corn, 110

Sweet & Tangy Corn Salad, 16

Dessert

Candy Bar Delight, 158

Isie's Lemon Fingers, 157

Peter's Apple Pie, 159

Dips

El Gato's Guacamole, 5

Please Pass the Hummus, 8

Duck

Crispy Roasted Whole Duck, 90

Irresistible Braised Duck Legs, 88

Eggs

Fish & Shellfish

Green Beans

Green Peppers

Kale

Lamb

Mushrooms

Pasta

Chicken Breast Pockets with Proscuitto, 83

Citrus Ginger Chicken Noodle Salad, 71

Decadent Beef Stroganoff, 41

Frank Loves Pasta Carbonara, 96

I Love Pasta Chicken Alfredo, 79

Mom's German Spaetzle, 146

Sizzlin' Stir-Fried Asian Beef & Noodles, 46

Wine Braised Short Ribs over Pasta, 50

Pork

Asian-Glazed Grilled Pork Tenderloin, 94

Cowboy Baby Back Ribs, 102

Delicioso Carnitas, 98

Dutch Sausage Rolls in Phyllo Dough, 12

Fourth of July South Carolina Style Pulled Pork, 100

Grandpa Carl's Sauerkraut & Keilbasa, 106

Herb Butter Bone-In Pork Chops, 104

Piquant Pork Schnitzel with Savory Mushroom Gravy, 92

Potatoes

A Taste of Germany Potato Pancakes, 149

Aunt Barb's German Potato Salad, 147

Grandma Doris' Potato Fritters, 134

Momma's Stuffed Bell Peppers with Creamy Mashed Potatoes, 60

Savory & Light Potato Gratin, 133

Salads

Caprese Salad with Toasted Baguette, 34

Chopped Salad with Goat Cheese Medallions, 36

Club House Wedge Salad, 24

Frank's Bacon Spinach Salad, 32

French Salad Lyonnaise, 22

Fresh Raspberry Salad, 20

Ginger Sesame Asian Slaw, 30

Greek Salad with Blackened Chicken, 28

Hail Kale Caesar Salad, 15

Restaurant Style Japanese Salad, 18

Savory Spinach & Creamy Gorgonzola Salad, 26

Sweet & Tangy Corn Salad, 16

Tangy English Cucumber Salad, 33

Side Dishes

Aunt Barb's German Potato Salad, 147

Frat Party Baked Beans, 138

Garden Fresh Spicy Yellow Squash, 137

Garlicky Kale, 139

Grandma Doris' Potato Fritters, 134

Indulgent Sweet Corn Pudding Souffle, 136

Mom's German Spaetzle, 146

Pancetta Roasted Brussel Sprouts, 140

Sauteed Balsamic Mushrooms, 144

Savory & Light Potato Gratin, 133

Spiced Sauteed Baby Bok Choy, 135

Tarragon Green Beans & Red Bell Peppers, 142

Soups

A Taste of Thai Curry Soup, 120

Baby It's Cold Outside Vietnamese Pho, 129

Finger Licking French Onion Soup, 125

Frank's Chinese Meatball Soup, 123

Sausage & Lentil Minestrone Soup, 127

Spinach

Frank's Bacon Spinach Salad, 32

Savory Spinach & Creamy Gorgonzola Salad, 26

Tomatoes

    Caprese Salad with Toasted Baguette, 37

ABOUT THE AUTHOR:

Janie May was born in Michigan to a Scottish mother, born and raised in Edinburgh. and a father with strong German lineage. She is a sibling to three brothers and one sister. Janie's parents were good people and taught her how to be a good person of good moral character. Some of Janie's fondest memories were those spent with her father, as a child. Janie's father taught her how to plant tulips, split and stack wood for the wood stove that heated their lake side home, and how to drive a 4 speed Corvette. He taught her so many things, that another book could be written; that's another story. Quite sadly, Janie's father succumbed to Leukemia at age 83. Her mother is still alive and well at 85. Janie attended one year of college at Western Michigan University and two years at the University of Anchorage. At 21 years old, Janie married her high school sweetheart who joined the Air Force and the two moved to San Antonio, Texas, where they spent 3 years. Janie and her then husband made a lifetime choice to live and be stationed in Anchorage, Alaska. They were married for 18 years before it became clear that it was not meant to be. Both Janie and her former husband continued to live in Alaska, and to this day, are still good friends.   Janie remained in Alaska from 1986 until 2016. After working for three years as a vocational counselor for people with disabilities, she worked as a Legal Investigator for a law firm for 30 years and finally retired at age 53.   She had planned to write a cookbook and her job was clearly getting in the way. Because she was tired of living in Alaska, with the snow, winter driving conditions, and a number of other things, she decided to make a move.   In November of 2016, Janie moved permanently to her vacation home in Glendale, Arizona.   It was quite a difference in climate, but she liked the "dry" heat (of course, it doesn't feel so dry when it is 118 degrees⋯.).   Janie then fell in love with a gentleman from Holland (Frank) and the two were married in November of 2017.   It was a bond that very few can imagine.   Because Frank was living in Holland when they met, it was a very long and rocky road to allow him to live legally in the states.   But as indicated above, the legal marriage finally occurred. Janie and Frank have one AKC yellow Labrador named Magnum (female and Maggie for short).   They both enjoy golf, tennis and socializing.   They will be together until death does them part.   Love, love.

www.ingramcontent.com/pod-product-compliance
Lightning Source LLC
Chambersburg PA
CBHW042016090426
42811CB00015B/1657

* 9 7 8 0 6 9 2 1 3 0 3 0 8 *